Entertain

To
Jane

From:
Brittany

Date:
12/25/11

Message:
Merry Christmas!

a THYME TO ENTERTAIN

Menus & Traditions of Annapolis

a THYME TO ENTERTAIN

Menus & Traditions of Annapolis

Published by The Junior League of Annapolis, Inc.

Cover and Food Photography © Dean Alexander

Food Photography Assistant: Sean Schwessinger

Food Stylist: Stephanie Rose

Food Styling Interns: Martina Bruno and Tricia Sawyer

Graphic Artist: Jodi Roberts

Page 211 is an extension of the copyright page.

This cookbook is a collection of favorite recipes,
which are not necessarily original recipes.

Library of Congress Control Number: 2007922894
ISBN: 978-0-9642139-1-3

Edited, Designed, and Manufactured
by **Favorite Recipes® Press**
An imprint of

FRP®

P. O. Box 305142, Nashville, Tennessee 37230
800-358-0560

Art Director: Steve Newman

Book Design: Dave Malone

Project Editor: Linda A. Jones

Manufactured in China
First Printing: 2007
15,000 copies

Photography on
pages 73, 119,
163, and 179
© Annapolis and
Anne Arundel
County Conference
and Visitors Bureau.

Photography on
pages 43, 59, 89,
103, 135, and 149
© The Baltimore Sun
Company.

Photography on
page 15 © Tinka.
Image from
BigStockPhoto.com.

Photography on
page 29
© Reynolds Tavern.

COOKBOOK COMMITTEES

2006-2007 COOKBOOK COMMITTEE MEMBERS

Meg Samek-Smith, *President*

Sandy Nuwar, *Advisor*

Stephanie Griffith, *Co-chair*   Hallie Wyrick, *Co-chair*

Wendy Bogarde	Amanda Finnis	Lisa Pickett
Lee Perry Casey	Kimberly Hilliard	Nikki Schieke
Angela Carbone-Clanton	Daphne Jenkins	Kat Spitzer
Ann Cole	Laura Lane	Colleen Wood
Tammy Counts	Kristi McCue	Allison Ekstrom*
Kelly Dovi	Anne Murphy	Emilia Poiter**
	Mandy Owens	

2005-2006 COOKBOOK COMMITTEE MEMBERS

Carole Mendez, *President*

Wendy Stam, *Advisor*

Wendy Bogarde, *Co-chair*   Allison Buckley, *Co-chair*   Hallie Wyrick, *Co-chair*

Ann Cole	Kimberly Hilliard	Nikki Schieke
Mary Diligent	Daphne Jenkins	Kat Spitzer
Stephanie Griffith		Lara Steinbach

2004-2005 INITIAL DEVELOPMENT COMMITTEE

Cheryl Kinney, *President*

Dana Cate	Kimberly Hilliard	Stephanie Reisinger
Allison Ekstrom*	Carole Mendez	Hallie Wyrick
	Elaina O'Toole	

* Sustainer Member

**The Junior League of Annapolis, Inc. Administrative Director

CONTENTS

CONTENTS

CONTENTS

CONTENTS

VISION

The Junior League of Annapolis, Inc. (JLA) is the leader in making our community a place where all children can reach their full potential.

MISSION

The Junior League of Annapolis, Inc. is an organization of women committed to promoting voluntarism, developing the potential of women, and improving the community through the effective action and leadership of trained volunteers. Its purpose is exclusively educational and charitable. It reaches out to all women of any race, religion, or national origin who demonstrate an interest in and a commitment to voluntarism. The Junior League of Annapolis, Inc. is part of the Association of Junior Leagues International, Inc.

VALUES

Helping Other People Through Meaningful Work

Leadership

Trained Volunteers

Honesty/Integrity/Ethical Practice

Commitment

Effectiveness

Forward Thinking

JUNIOR LEAGUE OF ANNAPOLIS, INC.
Women building better communities

FOREWORD

I am thrilled to be able to share with you my excitement as The Junior League of Annapolis presents this new cookbook. The title of this cookbook, *A Thyme to Entertain*, is truly indicative of the role that food plays in all our lives. Growing up in Lake City, South Carolina, life revolved around entertaining. My mother, a fabulous cook and a gracious entertainer, constantly entertained my father's customers with recipes that had been in our family for generations. There always seemed to be weekly cookouts on our terrace or delicious dinners with friends. Whether it was a planned cocktail party or a last-minute barbecue, I quickly learned the enjoyment food brought into everyone's lives.

I always looked forward to "Family Night Dinners" at my church when everyone contributed their best dishes. You always knew who brought the best deviled eggs, the best fried chicken, and the best cakes, of course. Food brought us all together in happy times and in sad. It was the core of our lives—the hospitality and the grace we learned to share.

My association with the Junior League began as a newly married woman in the Junior League of Washington, DC, and has continued with the Annapolis League since we moved here in 1976. As a Sustaining Member, I am very proud to be asked to write this foreword, as much that I have done in Annapolis has revolved around hospitality and entertaining.

You will see that the recipes in this cookbook carry on that tradition of hospitality and celebrate the events that we all share. While many of the happenings that are presented in this cookbook are particular to the Annapolis community, all of them can be reinterpreted to fit your celebration. I hope that you will thoroughly enjoy all the recipes and menu ideas and share with us any memories you may create.

All the best,

Caroline R. Reutter

Caroline R. Reutter

INTRODUCTION

Annapolitans are snuggled between two busy metropolitan areas and bustling beach destinations. Commuters travel to Washington, DC and Baltimore, MD, and beachgoers head out to the Atlantic Ocean, all within hours of each other. This wonderful combination has lead to a wide variety in lifestyles and events, which we have tried to share with you in this cookbook, *A Thyme to Entertain*.

The Junior League of Annapolis, Inc. (JLA) celebrated its 25th Anniversary in 2006. To mark this milestone, we felt it was appropriate to share our region, our traditions, and our events by bringing together this collection of recipes and menus in *A Thyme to Entertain*. The JLA focuses on promoting voluntarism, developing the potential of women, and improving the community through the effective action and leadership of trained volunteers in the local community.

Annapolis is the capital of the state of Maryland and the home of the United States Naval Academy, yet is still a quaint seaport village steeped in hundreds of years of maritime heritage. For over 300 years, Annapolis has been known for its cuisine and historic accommodations and as such, is a popular destination. A walk along the old brick sidewalks of the downtown streets conjures up images of the days of colonial Annapolis, when historic figures such as George Washington and Thomas Jefferson roamed the town. The city also boasts some of the finest architecture from the eighteenth and nineteenth centuries, including several buildings and residences open to the public. The City Dock, always the heart of the town, is a lovely place to people watch, shop and stroll, or tie up your boat. For lunch or dinner, the town's gastronomic choices are endless, from ice cream to crab.

As the New Year approaches, Annapolitans get in the holiday spirit by entertaining at home or attending festive holiday gatherings. The Annual Eastport Yacht Club Lights Parade is just one reason to gather and watch more than seventy boats lit up for the season float through Spa Creek to the delight of spectators. Spring is announced as the Naval Academy "Mids" and the St. John's College "Johnnies" square off in an annual croquet match on the campus's great lawn while spectators, dressed to the nines, share lavish champagne picnic spreads. And, we are treated to thoroughbred racing at local Steeplechases like The Roedown Races, where the competition for "Best Tailgate" is a strong event. May is ushered in by a spectacular May Day Celebration, which brings out inimitable displays of flowers and tea parties. In mid-spring, we hustle over to the Chesapeake Bay Bridge for our big chance to walk the 4.3-mile span across the Bay. Summer is marked by the flight of the Blue Angels over the Naval Academy's Commissioning week. It is a time for sailing in the self-proclaimed "Sailing Capital of the World" as well as a bounty of blue crabs, oysters, and rockfish, which inspire boat and backyard festivities. And as fall approaches, we look forward to football tailgate season, apple picking, visits to the pumpkin patch, and cool evenings spent by the fire.

All these events bring us opportunities to enjoy celebrating together with food, drink, and merriment. We have brought you several recipes in *A Thyme to Entertain*. We hope you'll delight in our traditions and menus as much as we do.

Meg Samek-Smith, President
The Junior League of Annapolis, Inc.

ENTERTAINING TIPS

When coming to a party, everyone loves the unexpected—have a make-your-own-ice-cream-sundae or a make-your-own-pizza-party for adults.

Start your party with a theme. It can be subtle like a color scheme or it can be over the top like a "Salute to Maryland" tailgate. The invitation will set the mood for your gathering. Consider making a creative invitation and hand deliver it. Some ideas:

- For a holiday gathering tie your invitation to a small live green wreath and hang it on the recipient's doorknob.
- For a nautical party, hang your invitation from tiny wooden sailboats, life rings, or other nautical items.
- For a tea, deliver your invitation in a vintage teacup. These are quite inexpensive at antique shops or flea markets.

Next, decorate inside and outside of your party venue. Guests will enjoy arriving when you welcome them in a special way. For example:

- For a crab feast, fill two crab bushels with potted seasonal flowers and place them on either side of your door.
- For a Mexican fiesta, hang a piñata from your flagpole.
- For a Fourth of July party, line the walkway with small American flags.

Carry your theme into your home or throughout the party area. Use containers instead of traditional vases for flower arrangements.

- Try tea bag tins, tea pots, and tea cups for a ladies' luncheon.
- Use crab seasoning tines, jelly/canning jars, baby food jars, and miniature pumpkins for other theme events.
- Tired of flowers? Use seashells, starfish, and sand dollars for a seashore party. They'll be beautiful in a glass vase.
- New paint cans from a hardware store for a house-warming party would be a fun flower container, or can be filled with paint brushes and stirrers.
- Try using edibles as centerpieces for a sit-down dinner. Nuts, candy, and fruit make a beautiful and delicious centerpiece.

ENTERTAINING TIPS

Finally, send your guests home with a favor to remember the occasion.

- A crab mallet with a little ribbon tied around it.
- For a cookie exchange party, send your guests home with a package of personalized recipe cards. You can easily make these on your computer.
- If your budget is large, consider having visors made to remember a special sporting event get-together.

Be creative!

WATER GOBLET

BUTTER SPREADER

DESSERT SPOON

WINE GLASS

BREAD & BUTTER PLATE

DESSERT FORK

DINNER FORK

SALAD FORK

DINNER KNIFE

DINNER PLATE

SOUP SPOON

NAPKIN

A GUIDE TO A PROPER PLACE SETTING

VINEYARD FARE

The expansive coastal plains of the Chesapeake Bay, the fertile rolling fields of the

Piedmont, the rich scenic plateau of the Allegany mountains—welcome to the diversity

and beauty of Maryland! Maryland's diverse regions are the perfect backdrop for a

wide variety of picturesque vineyards. And each year this diversity—of geography,

climate, and soil—provides our winemakers with a wonderfully unique and richly

varied harvest. From the mountains of Western Maryland to the Chesapeake plains,

from country landscapes to quaint historic towns, Maryland's wineries provide a wide

variety of delightful settings for a family adventure, a gathering with friends, a romantic

interlude, or a moment of quiet solitude.

Sponsored by
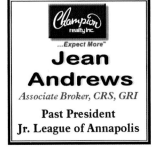

Vineyard Fare

Hot Mango Brie Cheese

Mushroom Tarts

Tomato Goat Cheese Napoleons

Cheese and Olive Spread

Caviar Spread

Feta and Pine Nut Orzo Salad

...a gathering of friends

Hot Mango Brie Cheese

Easy — Serves 8 to 10

1 (8-inch) round of Brie cheese

1 cup mango chutney or spicy
  mango chutney

8 slices bacon, crisp-cooked and
  crumbled

Place the cheese in a 10-inch quiche pan. Spread the chutney evenly over the top of the cheese and spread almost to the edge. Sprinkle the bacon on the top. Bake at 350 degrees for 30 to 45 minutes or until the chutney begins to bubble. Serve with bread or crackers. (Note: For a vegetarian variation, substitute 1/2 cup toasted slivered almonds for the bacon.)

Mushroom Tarts

Moderate — Makes 2 dozen

24 slices white bread

1/4 cup (1/2 stick) butter or
  margarine, melted

1/4 cup minced green onions

1/4 cup (1/2 stick) butter or
  margarine, melted

8 ounces mushrooms, finely chopped

2 tablespoons all-purpose flour

1 cup whipping cream

4 1/2 teaspoons minced chives

1 tablespoon minced fresh parsley

1/2 teaspoon lemon juice

1/2 teaspoon salt

1/8 teaspoon red pepper

Grated Parmesan cheese

Cut a round from each slice of the bread with a 3-inch biscuit cutter. Brush miniature muffin cups with some of 1/4 cup butter. Gently fit the bread rounds into the muffin cups. Brush the bread with the remaining 1/4 cup butter. Bake at 400 degrees for 10 minutes or until light brown. Cool completely in the pan.

Sauté the green onions in 1/4 cup butter in a large heavy skillet for 1 minute. Stir in the mushrooms. Cook, uncovered, for 10 minutes, stirring occasionally. Remove from the heat and stir in the flour. Add the cream gradually, stirring to incorporate. Bring to a boil over medium heat and boil for 1 minute or until the mixture thickens. Remove from the heat and stir in the chives, parsley, lemon juice, salt and red pepper. Spoon the mushroom mixture evenly into the bread cups and sprinkle with cheese. Bake at 350 degrees for 10 minutes. Serve immediately.

A Thyme to Entertain

Tomato Goat Cheese Napoleons

Easy — Serves 4

Core the top of the tomatoes. Cut each tomato horizontally into four even slices, keeping the slices in order of top to bottom. Drain the slices of excess liquid on paper towels. Arrange the goat cheese evenly over the three bottom slices of each tomato. Top the goat cheese evenly with the pesto. Reassemble each tomato and secure with the rosemary sprigs speared through the center of the tomatoes. Chill, covered, in the refrigerator.

To serve, place the tomatoes on a bed of mixed salad greens and drizzle with the balsamic vinaigrette. (Note: The napoleons, as a side dish, pair well with beef and lamb. This recipe can easily be doubled or tripled. You can use homemade pesto and homemade balsamic vinaigrette, if desired. For a beautiful presentation, use different colored tomatoes and mix the color slices when stacking.)

Photograph for this recipe appears on page 17.

4 small to medium tomatoes

4 ounces goat cheese or feta cheese

1 (8-ounce) jar basil pesto

4 (5-inch) sprigs of
    woody-stemmed rosemary

1 (8-ounce) bottle balsamic vinaigrette

Mixed salad greens or baby
    spinach leaves (optional)

Maryland wines are made with the grapes harvested from an estimated 250 acres of vineyards across the state. The twenty-five licensed wineries in the state produce over 180 different wines.

Cheese and Olive Spread

Easy — Serves 8 to 10

8 ounces cream cheese, softened

1/2 cup light mayonnaise

8 ounces Cheddar cheese,
   finely shredded

1/4 cup chopped green onions

1/4 cup chopped stuffed green olives,
   or to taste

2 tablespoons lemon juice

1/2 teaspoon red pepper, or to taste

Combine the cream cheese and mayonnaise in a bowl and blend until smooth. Stir in the Cheddar cheese, green onions, olives, lemon juice and red pepper. Chill, covered, until ready to serve. Serve with crackers and vegetables.

Caviar Spread

Easy — Serves 10 to 12

8 ounces cream cheese, softened

1/2 cup sour cream

1 tablespoon finely chopped
   green onions

1 garlic clove, minced

1 teaspoon onion flakes

2 ounces red caviar

Blend the cream cheese and sour cream in a bowl until smooth. Stir in the green onions, garlic and onion flakes. Fold in the caviar. Chill, covered, until ready to serve. Serve with crackers.

A Thyme to Entertain

Feta and Pine Nut Orzo Salad

Easy — Serves 10 to 12

Cook the orzo in a 6- to 8-quart pot of boiling salted water until tender; drain well. Toast the pine nuts in a sauté pan over low heat until golden brown and fragrant. Whisk the lemon juice, olive oil, salt and pepper in a bowl. Add the hot orzo and toss to coat. Fold in the pine nuts, feta cheese and scallions. Season with salt and pepper.

1 pound orzo

Salt to taste

1/2 cup pine nuts

1/4 cup lemon juice

1/4 cup olive oil

Pepper to taste

1 1/4 cups crumbled feta cheese

1 cup thinly sliced scallions

Annapolitan's Sangria

Moderate — Serves 4 to 6

Combine the brandy and sugar in a large pitcher and stir until the sugar is dissolved. Stir in the lemon, lime and orange slices. Let stand at room temperature for 1 hour. Stir in the wine and lime juice and chill for 1 hour. Stir in the club soda and serve in large chilled wine glasses. Garnish with additional lime or lemon slices.

1/2 cup brandy

1/4 cup sugar

1 lemon, thinly sliced

1 lime, thinly sliced

1 orange, thinly sliced

1 (750-milliliter) bottle red wine

Juice of 1 lime

1 quart club soda, chilled

Lime slices and lemon slices

Cranberry Chutney and Goat Cheese

Moderate — Serves 10 to 12

1 large baguette

1 onion, thinly sliced

1 cup packed dark brown sugar

1 cup water

2 Granny Smith apples, peeled and
   cut into 1/4-inch pieces

3/4 cup apple cider vinegar

1 1/2 teaspoons grated fresh ginger

1/2 teaspoon salt

1/2 teaspoon mustard seeds

Grated zest and juice of 1 lime

Grated zest and juice of 1 orange

1/3 cup currants

3 cups cranberries

1/2 teaspoon cardamom

1/2 teaspoon curry powder

1/4 teaspoon cayenne pepper

12 ounces goat cheese

Sprigs of fresh rosemary

Slice the baguette horizontally into twenty-four slices. Place on a baking sheet and bake at 350 degrees until crisp and light golden brown. Combine the onion, brown sugar and water in large saucepan. Bring to a simmer and simmer for 20 minutes or until the onion is tender. Stir in the apples, vinegar, ginger, salt, mustard seeds, lime zest and orange zest. Return to a simmer and simmer for 10 minutes. Stir in the lime juice, orange juice, currants, cranberries, cardamom, curry powder and cayenne pepper. Return to a simmer and simmer for 15 minutes or until the cranberries begin to split open. Chill, covered, until ready to serve. Spread the chutney over the goat cheese and serve with the baguette slices on the side. Garnish with sprigs of rosemary.

The Maryland Wine Festival has been an annual event for more than twenty years. It started as a small amateur festival for people to get comments on their homemade wine and to sample varieties from different Maryland vineyards. It has grown now into the premier wine festival in the state, with all of the state's wineries participating annually, and includes the Governor's Cup Competition and the Amateur Wine Competition.

A Thyme to Entertain

Cheddar Biscuits

Moderate — Makes 12 to 16 biscuits

Combine the flour, baking powder, sugar, cream of tartar, cayenne pepper and salt in a bowl and mix well. Work in the butter by hand until crumbly. Stir in the cheese. Make a well in the center of the flour mixture and add the milk. Stir with a fork working from the center of the well outward until the flour mixture comes together. Do not overmix. Turn out onto a lightly floured surface and knead gently 10 to 12 times. Pat the dough into a 1/2-inch-thick circle. Cut with a 2-inch biscuit cutter and place on a lightly buttered baking sheet. Bake at 425 degrees for 12 to 15 minutes or until golden brown. These are best served hot from the oven.

2 cups unbleached all-purpose flour

4 teaspoons baking powder

1 tablespoon sugar

1/2 teaspoon cream of tartar

1/2 teaspoon cayenne pepper, or to taste

1 teaspoon salt

1/2 cup (1 stick) unsalted butter, cut into small pieces

1 cup (4 ounces) shredded sharp Cheddar cheese

2/3 cup milk

By experimenting with different varieties and growing conditions, the Maryland wine industry slowly grew throughout the 19th century. However, it only achieved real success when Philip Wagner, a local newspaper editor, planted as many different hybrids as he could at his Baltimore County home. In short, they prospered, and soon Wagner was producing his own wine and selling the vines throughout the East coast. In 1945 he opened Maryland's first bonded winery, Boordy Vineyards, which is still in operation today under the ownership of the R.B. Deford family.

Festive Shrimp with Couscous

Moderate — Serves 4

1¹/2 pounds medium shrimp, peeled
   and deveined

Coarse salt and pepper to taste

2 tablespoons olive oil

1 teaspoon brown mustard seeds

2 leeks, sliced into ¹/2-inch
   half moons

2 carrots, shredded

5 garlic cloves, thinly sliced

1 cup couscous

1 cup frozen or fresh peas, blanched

2 cups boiling water

Season the shrimp with salt and pepper. Sauté the shrimp in 1 tablespoon of the hot olive oil in a 12-inch skillet for 3 minutes or until the shrimp turn pink and are cooked through. Remove the shrimp from the skillet; set aside. Add the remaining 1 tablespoon olive oil to the skillet. Stir in the mustard seeds and cook for 30 seconds or until the seeds begin to pop. Add the leeks, carrots and garlic. Sauté for 5 minutes or until the leeks are tender. Stir in the couscous, peas, boiling water, salt and pepper. Remove from the heat. Cover with a tight-fitting lid and let stand for 5 minutes. Fold in the shrimp. Adjust the seasonings.

Poppy Seed Chicken

Easy — Serves 4 to 6

2 (10-ounce) cans cream of
   chicken soup

¹/4 cup sour cream

¹/4 cup milk

3 cups chopped cooked chicken

2 tablespoons poppy seeds,
   or to taste

Salt and pepper to taste

1 sleeve (4 ounces) butter
   crackers, crushed

2 teaspoons butter, melted

Combine the soup and sour cream in a bowl and mix until smooth. Stir in the milk. Add the chicken and poppy seeds and mix well. Spoon the mixture into a baking dish. Top with the crackers and then drizzle with the butter. Bake at 350 degrees for 45 minutes. Let stand for 10 minutes. Serve with rice.

Tomatoes and Basil

Easy — Serves 4 to 6

Combine the tomatoes, olive oil, garlic, basil and sugar in a bowl and mix well. Season with salt and pepper. Spoon the mixture into a glass jar or bowl and seal with a tight-fitting lid. Let stand in the direct sunlight for 5 to 6 hours. Serve over hot cooked pasta.

5 or 6 large tomatoes,
    coarsely chopped

1/2 cup olive oil

6 garlic cloves, minced

1 handful of basil leaves, torn

1 tablespoon sugar

Salt and freshly ground pepper to taste

Hot cooked pasta or hot toasted
    Italian bread

Ratatouille

Easy — Serves 10 to 12

Place the zucchini and eggplant in a colander and sprinkle with 1 teaspoon salt. Weigh down the mixture with a heavy object and place the colander in a sink for 1 hour for the bitter juices to drain. Dry the zucchini and eggplant with a tea towel. Arrange the zucchini, eggplant, tomatoes, bell peppers and onion evenly in a roasting pan. Sprinkle with the garlic and basil. Toss with the olive oil to coat. Season with salt and pepper to taste. Place on the highest oven rack and roast at 450 degrees for 30 to 40 minutes or until the vegetables are brown around the edges. Serve immediately or at room temperature.

2 zucchini, coarsely chopped

1 eggplant, coarsely chopped

1 teaspoon salt

1 pound cherry tomatoes

1 red bell pepper, chopped into
    1-inch pieces

1 yellow bell pepper, chopped into
    1-inch pieces

1 onion, coarsely chopped

2 teaspoons chopped garlic

1 handful of basil leaves, chopped

3 tablespoons olive oil

Salt and freshly ground pepper
    to taste

Apple-Glazed Cheddar Cheesecake

Gourmet — Serves 10

Cheddar Cheesecake

1 cup crushed cinnamon graham
  crackers or crushed gingersnaps

1/3 cup finely chopped pecans

3 tablespoons butter, melted

1/8 teaspoon orange extract

24 ounces cream cheese, softened

3/4 cup (3 ounces) finely shredded
  sharp or extra-sharp Cheddar
  cheese

3/4 cup sugar

3 tablespoons all-purpose flour

1/2 teaspoon grated orange zest

1/8 teaspoon grated lemon zest

4 eggs

1 egg yolk

3/4 cup sour cream

Apple Glaze

1/2 cups frozen apple juice concentrate

1 teaspoon lemon juice

4 teaspoons cornstarch

Grated or chopped zest of 1 orange

1/4 teaspoon cinnamon

1/8 teaspoon ginger

3 cups thinly sliced peeled Granny
  Smith apples

1 teaspoon butter

1/4 teaspoon vanilla extract

1/4 to 1/3 cup chopped pecans, toasted

To prepare the cheesecake, combine the graham crackers, pecans, butter and orange extract in a bowl and mix well. Press firmly over the bottom and up the side of a 9-inch springform pan. Bake at 350 degrees for 5 minutes. Remove from the oven to cool completely. Increase the oven temperature to 450 degrees. Beat the cream cheese in a large mixing bowl, or process in a food processor, until smooth and creamy. Add the Cheddar cheese and beat well. Beat in the sugar and flour. Add the orange zest and the lemon zest and mix well. Add the eggs one at a time, mixing well after each addition. Beat in the egg yolk. Add the sour cream and mix well. Pour the filling into the cooled crust. Bake for 10 minutes. Reduce the oven temperature to 300 degrees and bake for 1 hour longer. Turn off the oven and open the oven door. Let the cheesecake cool in the oven for 1 to 10 hours. (Note: You may substitute chopped hazelnuts or almonds for the pecans.)

To prepare the glaze, combine the apple juice concentrate, lemon juice, cornstarch, orange zest, cinnamon and ginger in a saucepan and bring to a boil. Cook until thickened, stirring constantly. Add the apples and butter. Simmer until the apples are transparent and tender but not mushy. Stir in the vanilla and pecans. Chill, covered, until the glaze thickens further. Spoon over the cheesecake and chill for 6 to 10 hours.

A Thyme to Entertain

Chocolate Espresso Cake with Raspberry Sauce

Moderate — Serves 20

Combine the semisweet chocolate and the unsweetened chocolate in a large heatproof bowl. Bring the butter, espresso and brown sugar to a boil in a saucepan, stirring constantly until the sugar dissolves. Add the espresso mixture to the chocolate and whisk until smooth. Cool slightly. Whisk in the eggs. Pour the batter into a 9-inch cake pan lined on the bottom with baking parchment. Place the cake pan in a larger baking pan. Add enough hot water to the larger pan to come halfway up the sides of the cake pan. Bake at 350 degrees for 1 hour or until the center of the cake is set and a cake tester inserted into the center comes out with a few moist crumbs attached. Remove the cake pan from the water. Chill, covered, for 8 to 10 hours. Process the raspberries in a food processor in batches until puréed. Strain the purée into a bowl and chill until ready to serve, discarding the solids. (The sauce can be made up to two days ahead if desired.)

Run a knife around the side of the cake to loosen from the pan. Hold the cake pan over low heat for 15 seconds or until the bottom of the pan is slightly warm. Invert onto a serving plate. Remove the pan and carefully peel off the baking parchment. Serve with the raspberry sauce and garnish with fresh raspberries. (Note: You may use 1 tablespoon instant espresso powder dissolved in 1 cup water for the freshly brewed espresso.)

12 ounces semisweet chocolate, coarsely chopped

4 ounces unsweetened chocolate, coarsely chopped

2 cups (4 sticks) unsalted butter, cut into small pieces

1 cup freshly brewed espresso

1 cup packed light brown sugar

8 eggs, lightly beaten

3 (10-ounce) packages frozen raspberries in syrup, thawed

Fresh raspberries

A CUP OF ANNAPOLIS

A tea can be a time for women to dust off their finest china and polish their silver, or it can be a perfectly casual afternoon in the garden with mismatched antique tea cups.

To set the table, here are a few suggestions:

• Use a multilayered server or platter to display the different types of pastries or sandwiches. Offer both savory and sweet foods, including: savory tarts, small finger sandwiches, tea cakes, pastries, scones, and cookies.

• Have dishes of whipped or clotted cream and various preserves set out on the table.

• Serve a one-person pot of tea to each guest. Use colorful teacups and saucers (they can be elegantly mismatched).

• As center pieces, use multiple teacups and teapots as flowerpots, holding flower blooms cut short so that there are not a lot of stems showing. Arrange them in clusters in the middle of the table.

Now's the time to bring out your prettiest trays for serving.

Reynolds Tavern

Sponsored by

A Cup of Annapolis

Blue Cheese Nibbles

Popovers with Strawberry Butter

Chilled Zucchini Soup

Eastern Shore Chicken Salad

Egg Salad with Bacon

White Chocolate Cranberry Scones

...a perfectly casual afternoon in the garden

Blue Cheese Nibbles

Easy — Serves 6 to 8

1 (10-count) package
    refrigerator biscuits
1/4 cup (1/2 stick) butter
1/4 cup crumbled blue cheese
1 teaspoon Worcestershire sauce

Cut each biscuit into quarters and arrange in a baking pan with sides touching. Melt the butter and cheese in a saucepan, stirring occasionally. Stir in the Worcestershire sauce. Pour the cheese mixture over the biscuits. Bake at 400 degrees for 12 to 15 minutes or until golden brown. Serve hot.

There are four main categories of tea, all of which originate from the tea plant. Black tea, the most common, is fermented by exposing the leaves to air for a prescribed amount of time, then heating and drying them, resulting in a dark color and a full, rich flavor. Green tea leaves are dried but not fermented; the tea they produce is light green in color, with a mild, grassy flavor. Oolong tea is semifermented and has a taste between that of black and green teas. White tea is difficult to find outside of China, where it is produced; it is a delicate tea made of only the leaf tips and buds of the tea plant.

Popovers with Strawberry Butter

Easy — Serves 12

To prepare the strawberry butter, blend the butter and preserves in a bowl until smooth.

To prepare the popovers, beat the eggs and milk in a mixing bowl until frothy. Add the flour and salt and beat for 1 minute or until large bubbles form. Let stand at room temperature for 30 to 45 minutes. Beat again for 1 minute or until large bubbles form. Liberally coat twelve muffin cups with butter. Fill each cup two-thirds full with the batter. Bake at 400 degrees for 35 to 40 minutes or until the popovers swell up and are golden brown. Do not open the oven door while baking. Remove from the oven and immediately pierce the tops with a knife to relieve the steam. Serve warm with the strawberry butter.

Strawberry Butter

1/2 cup (1 stick) salted butter, softened

1/2 cup strawberry preserves

Popovers

2 eggs

1 cup milk

1 cup all-purpose flour

1/2 teaspoon salt

Butter for coating

Chilled Zucchini Soup

Easy — Serves 4 to 5

1 onion, chopped

1/2 cup (1 stick) butter, melted

11/2 pounds zucchini, peeled
    and shredded

21/2 cups low-sodium chicken broth

1 cup heavy cream

1 teaspoon dried basil

1 teaspoon freshly ground pepper

1 teaspoon salt

1/2 teaspoon freshly grated nutmeg

Zucchini slices

Sauté the onion in the butter in a skillet until tender. Stir in the zucchini and chicken broth and bring to a simmer. Simmer for 15 minutes. Process the mixture in a food processor until puréed. Add the cream, basil, pepper, salt and nutmeg and pulse to mix well. Chill, covered, for 8 to 10 hours. To serve, spoon into individual serving bowls and garnish with zucchini slices.

Photograph for this recipe appears on page 31.

Eastern Shore Chicken Salad

Moderate — Serves 6 to 8

6 boneless skinless chicken breasts

2 green onions, sliced

1 cup almonds, toasted and crushed

11/2 cups red seedless grapes, sliced
    into halves lengthwise

1 cup crumbled blue cheese,
    such as Gorgonzola

1/2 cup mayonnaise, or to taste

Salt and pepper to taste

Boil the chicken in water to cover for 1 hour; drain, discarding the liquid. Let stand to cool. Shred the chicken with a fork or process in a food processor. Place the chicken in a large bowl. Fold in the green onions, almonds, grapes, cheese and mayonnaise until well combined. Season with salt and pepper. Serve on a bed of lettuce or miniature croissants.

A Thyme to Entertain

Egg Salad with Bacon

Easy — Serves 8 to 10

Cut the bacon into 1-inch pieces and fry in a skillet until crisp; drain. Combine the bacon, eggs, celery, scallions, mayonnaise, horseradish and caraway seeds in a bowl and mix well. Season with salt and pepper. Garnish with the parsley and serve as a salad or open-faced on Pumpernickel bread.

12 ounces bacon

1 dozen eggs, hard-cooked
    and chopped

6 ribs celery, chopped

5 scallions, chopped

1 cup mayonnaise

3 to 4 tablespoons
    horseradish, drained

2 tablespoons caraway seeds

Salt and pepper to taste

1/2 cup fresh parsley, chopped

Sliced Pumpernickel bread (optional)

In 2001 The Junior League of Annapolis, Inc. formed Teen Empowerment And Mentoring—the TEAM project. The purpose of the project was to develop a suite of programs in Anne Arundel County to encourage female teens to reach their full potential. The first project was a partnership with Anne Arundel Medical Center to assist with teen birthing classes and to provide basic life skills programming to teen mothers and their children. In 2006 that partnership expanded to include administering GoGirlGo!, a project designed by The Women's Sports Foundation, which combines physical activity with educational intervention focusing on reducing and preventing health-risk behaviors. In partnership with the YWCA of Anne Arundel County's Family Support Center and its Interagency Coalition on Adolescent Pregnancy Prevention and Parenting Program, TEAM volunteers have also worked on administering a peer-to-peer pregnancy prevention program.

White Chocolate Cranberry Scones

Moderate — Makes 16 scones

3 cups all-purpose flour

1/4 cup granulated sugar

4 teaspoons baking powder

1/2 teaspoon salt

3/4 cup (1 1/2 sticks) butter, chilled
    and cut into small pieces

2 eggs, lightly beaten

1 cup heavy cream or milk

1/2 cup (3 ounces) white
    chocolate chips

1/4 cup dried cranberries

2 tablespoons milk

Granulated sugar or Turbinado
    sugar for sprinkling

Combine the flour, 1/4 cup sugar, baking powder and salt in a bowl and mix well. Cut in the butter by hand until crumbly. Stir in the eggs and cream. Stir in the white chocolate chips and cranberries. Turn out the dough onto a floured surface. Pat the dough into a 1-inch-thick square. Brush the top of the dough with the milk and sprinkle the top with additional sugar. Cut the dough into four squares. Cut each of the four squares diagonally into four triangles. Place on a baking sheet. Bake at 375 degrees for 15 minutes or until golden brown and cooked through. Serve warm with jam and whipped cream.

A Thyme to Entertain

Sunshine Punch

Easy — Serves 15

Fill a ring mold with 2 quarts orange juice and freeze until solid. Combine the remaining 2 quarts orange juice, the lemonade and pineapple juice in a large punch bowl and mix well. Stir in the lemon-lime soda. Add the frozen orange juice ring and ice as needed. Serve immediately.

1 gallon (4 quarts) orange juice

2 quarts lemonade

1 (46-ounce) can pineapple juice

1 (2-liter) bottle lemon-lime soda

Tomato Tart

Easy — Serves 6 to 8

Sauté the green onions in the butter in a small skillet until tender-crisp; do not brown. Remove from the heat and cool slightly. Combine the cheese and flour in a bowl and mix well; set aside. Spray a 9-inch pie plate or tart pan with a removable bottom lightly with nonstick cooking spray. Unfold the pie pastry and fit it into the prepared pie plate. Spread the cheese mixture in the bottom of the pie shell. Top with the basil and oregano and slightly mix them into the cheese mixture. Spread the green onions on top of the herbs. Arrange the tomatoes slices on top so that they overlap. Sprinkle with salt and pepper. Bake at 375 degrees for 25 to 30 minutes or until the tomatoes are tender. Serve warm or at room temperature. (Note: You may use 1 teaspoon dried basil instead of fresh basil.)

1/2 cup thinly sliced green onions

1 tablespoon butter, melted

2 cups shredded Gruyère cheese or
    crumbled feta cheese

2 tablespoons all-purpose flour

1 refrigerator pie pastry

1/4 cup finely chopped fresh basil

1/4 cup finely chopped fresh oregano

3 ripe tomatoes, sliced horizontally
    into 1/4-inch rounds

Salt and pepper to taste

Miniature Breakfast Quiches

Easy — Serves 8 to 10

1 (6-ounce) container garlic and herb
    cheese spread

1/2 cup milk

2 eggs, lightly beaten

1 tablespoon chopped fresh
    chives (optional)

30 miniature phyllo shells

Mix the cheese, milk, eggs and chives together in a bowl until smooth. Spoon the mixture evenly into the phyllo shells. Bake at 375 degrees for 8 to 10 minutes or until the filling is set and the phyllo shells are golden brown.

Pecan-Crusted Artichoke and Cheese Spread

Easy — Serves 15 to 20

1 onion, chopped

2 garlic cloves, minced

3 tablespoons butter or
    margarine, melted

4 cups coarsely chopped spinach

1 (13-ounce) can artichoke hearts,
    drained and chopped

8 ounces cream cheese, cut into pieces

8 ounces four-cheese blend, shredded

3/4 cup (3 ounces) shredded
    Parmesan cheese

1/2 cup mayonnaise

2/3 cup chopped pecans

1/2 cup herb-seasoned stuffing mix

1 tablespoon butter or
    margarine, melted

Sauté the onion and garlic in 3 tablespoons butter in a large skillet until tender. Add the spinach and cook over medium heat for 3 minutes, stirring frequently. Add the artichoke hearts, cream cheese, four-cheese blend, Parmesan cheese and mayonnaise and heat until the cheese melts, stirring constantly. Spoon the mixture into a 2-quart baking dish. Bake at 350 degrees for 20 minutes; stir gently. Combine the pecans, stuffing mix, and 1 tablespoon butter; toss until well combined. Sprinkle over the top of the cheese mixture and bake 15 minutes longer. Serve warm with pita chips, French bread or crackers. (Note: You may substitute Monterey Jack cheese for the four-cheese blend.)

A Thyme to Entertain

Warm-Your-Soul Soup

Easy — Serves 6 to 8

Combine the peas, ham, onion, carrots and celery in a slow cooker. Stir in the water and season with pepper. Cook on low for 8 to 10 hours or until tender. Stir well and ladle into broad-rimmed soup bowls. Serve with crusty bread or garlic cheese bread.

1 (16-ounce) package dry green peas

2 cups chopped ham

1 cup sliced onions

1 cup sliced carrots

1 cup sliced celery

6 cups water

Pepper to taste

Spinach Soup

Easy — Serves 4 to 6

Sauté the green onions in the butter in a stockpot until tender. Add the broth and bring to a boil. Stir in the half-and-half gradually. Add the potatoes, carrots and rice and bring to a simmer. Simmer for 15 minutes. Add the spinach and return to a simmer for 15 minutes longer. Stir in the salt.

1 cup chopped green onions

3 to 4 tablespoons butter, melted

46 ounces chicken broth

2 cups half-and-half

2 potatoes, sliced paper thin

2 carrots, sliced paper thin

1/4 cup rice

1 (10-ounce) package frozen
    chopped spinach, thawed
    and drained

1 teaspoon salt

Fanned Chicken with Tomato Basil Sauce

Easy — Serves 4

2 cups chicken stock

1/2 cup loosely packed fresh
   basil leaves

4 (8-ounce) boneless skinless
   chicken breasts

1 garlic clove

1 1/2 cups loosely packed fresh
   basil leaves

1/2 cup water

2 teaspoons mayonnaise
   (preferably homemade)

1 tomato, peeled, seeded
   and chopped

4 large basil leaves

Combine the stock and 1/2 cup basil leaves in a stockpot. Bring to a simmer over medium-low heat and simmer for 5 minutes. Add the chicken and gently poach, covered, for 8 minutes. Turn the chicken over and continue to poach for 4 minutes or until the chicken is cooked through and firm; set aside and keep warm.

Process the garlic in a food processor or blender until chopped. Add 1 1/2 cups basil and the water. Process the mixture until puréed. Pour into a fine mesh strainer lined with a paper towel. Press the mixture with the back of a spoon to remove excess water.

Scrape the drained basil purée into a bowl. Stir in the mayonnaise and half the tomato.

Remove the chicken from the poaching liquid, discarding the liquid, and pat dry. Slice each chicken breast on the diagonal. Arrange one large basil leaf on each of four dinner plates and place one sliced chicken breast on each leaf. Spread the slices into a fan pattern. Spoon the sauce between the slices of chicken. Sprinkle the remaining chopped tomato over the sauce.

A Thyme to Entertain

Pecan Blondies

Easy — Makes 2 dozen

Blend the biscuit mix, brown sugar and eggs in a bowl until smooth. Stir in the pecans. Pour the batter into a lightly greased 9x13-inch baking pan. Bake at 325 degrees for 35 to 40 minutes or until the blondies test done. Cool completely and then slice into 2-inch squares.

2 cups all-purpose biscuit mix
1 (1-pound) package light
 brown sugar
4 eggs, lightly beaten
2 cups chopped pecan

Sugar Cookies

Moderate — Makes 2 dozen

Combine the flour, baking soda and cream of tartar; set aside. Cream the butter, shortening, 1/2 cup granulated sugar and the confectioners' sugar in a mixing bowl until light and fluffy. Beat in the egg and flavorings. Add the flour mixture and mix well. Shape the dough into 1-inch balls and roll in granulated sugar. Arrange on a cookie sheet and flatten with the bottom of a beverage glass. Bake at 350 degrees for 8 minutes or until the edges are very light brown. Be careful not to overbake. (Note: The cookies are very delicate. They will freeze well separated with sheets of wax paper and placed in an airtight container. For special occasions, roll in colored sugar, such as pink for Easter or red and green for Christmas.)

2 cups all-purpose flour
1 teaspoon baking soda
1 teaspoon cream of tartar
1/2 cup (1 stick) butter or margarine
1/2 cup shortening
1/2 cup granulated sugar
1/2 cup confectioners' sugar
1 egg
1 teaspoon almond extract
1 teaspoon vanilla extract
Granulated sugar for coating

PICNIC

STEEPLECHASE

Horse racing can be found on Maryland's beautiful countryside and in the bustling cities. Horse racing in Maryland dates back to the 1800s. Maryland is known for Steeplechase, Roedown, and Preakness. These are only a few of the most popular races. These events bring in visitors from all over the country to watch such amazing Thoroughbreds.

Steeplechase racing is fun to watch as the horses jump through Maryland's countryside on wonderful spring days. It is easy to spot the winner; it's the first horse to cross the finish line. The first Maryland Steeplechase was run at Pimlico Race Track on October 18, 1873; races often arose as competitions between local fox hunting clubs.

Sponsored by

The Junior League of Annapolis, Inc. Sustainers

Steeplechase Picnic

DAFFODIL DIP • AVOCADO BRUSCHETTA

SPA CREEK SHRIMP CAKES

FIRST-PRIZE BEAN SALSA • MARINATED ASPARAGUS

LEMON JELL-O CAKE

...on Maryland's beautiful countryside

Daffodil Dip

Easy — Serves 10 to 12

1 hard-cooked egg

8 ounces cream cheese, softened

1/2 cup mayonnaise

2 tablespoons chopped fresh parsley

2 tablespoons chopped onion

1 garlic clove, minced

1/2 teaspoon salt

Dash of pepper

Peel the egg and separate the egg white from the yolk. Chop the egg white. Combine the cream cheese and mayonnaise in a bowl and mix well. Stir in the parsley. Add the egg white, onion, garlic, salt and pepper and mix well. Spoon into a serving bowl. Crumble the egg yolk over the top. Chill, covered, in the refrigerator. Serve with crackers or fresh vegetables. (Note: You may serve by spooning the dip evenly into ten to twelve endive leaves.)

Photograph for this recipe appears on page 45.

For a steeplechase or horse race party, have a children's area where children make their own stick ponies. Cut out pony heads from felt and attach them to wooden dowels. Let the children decorate them with colors of the "silks" and then have a race.

Sponsored by *National Carpet*

Avocado Bruschetta

Easy — Makes 3 dozen

Blend the lime juice, vinegar, 1 tablespoon olive oil, the hot sauce, garlic powder, 1/2 teaspoon salt and the white pepper in a bowl. Add the avocados, tomatoes and green onions and toss gently to coat. Cover and chill for 2 hours.

Combine 3 tablespoons olive oil, 1/2 teaspoon salt and the garlic in a small bowl and mix well. Place the bread slices on a baking sheet and brush evenly with the olive oil mixture. Bake at 350 degrees for 10 minutes or until toasted. Remove from the oven to cool.

To serve, top each toasted bread slice evenly with the avocado mixture and sprinkle with cilantro.

2 tablespoons fresh lime juice

1 tablespoon white wine vinegar

1 tablespoon olive oil

2 teaspoons hot sauce

1/2 teaspoon garlic powder

1/2 teaspoon salt

1/4 teaspoon white pepper

2 or 3 avocados, cut into cubes

2 plum tomatoes, seeded
    and chopped

2 or 3 green onions, chopped

3 tablespoons olive oil

1/2 teaspoon salt

1 or 2 garlic cloves, minced

36 slices French baguette
    (about 1 or 2 loaves)

Chopped fresh cilantro

When entertaining for a racing event make sure your table decor is upscale. Use your best linens, china, and silver. Pour drinks into your finest crystal glasses. Ladies, don't forget your finest hats. Men should wear seersucker suits and leave their socks at home.

Spa Creek Shrimp Cakes

Moderate — Serves 8

Lemon Vinaigrette

1 cup olive oil

1/4 cup fresh lemon juice

2/3 cup chopped fresh chives or
green onions

3 tablespoons finely chopped shallots

Shrimp Cakes

36 fresh asparagus spears

Salt to taste

2 tablespoons unsalted butter, melted

2/3 cup chopped shallots

1 1/2 pounds shrimp, peeled, deveined
and finely chopped

1 1/2 cups fresh white bread crumbs

1 red bell pepper, finely chopped

2 eggs, beaten

1/4 cup chopped fresh chives or
green onions

Pepper to taste

2 tablespoons unsalted butter, melted

To prepare the vinaigrette, whisk the olive oil, lemon juice, chives and shallots in a bowl until combined.

To prepare the shrimp cakes, trim the asparagus and cut into 6-inch pieces. Cook in boiling salted water in a saucepan for 3 minutes or until tender-crisp; drain. Rinse in cold water to stop the cooking process; drain well. Finely chop four of the asparagus spears, reserving the remaining asparagus spears. Melt 2 tablespoons butter in a heavy skillet over medium heat. Add the shallots and sauté for 2 minutes. Combine the sautéed shallots, chopped asparagus, shrimp, bread crumbs, bell pepper, eggs and chives in a bowl and mix well. Do not overmix. Season generously with salt and pepper. Shape the mixture into 3 1/2- to 4-inch rounds. Cook the shrimp cakes in batches in 2 tablespoons butter in a heavy nonstick skillet over medium heat for 5 minutes per side or until golden brown and cooked through.

To serve, arrange four of the reserved asparagus spears on each plate, overlapping at the corners to form squares. Top each with one shrimp cake. Spoon some of the vinaigrette over the top. Serve with the remaining vinaigrette.

Photograph for this recipe appears on page 45.

A Thyme to Entertain

First-Prize Bean Salsa

Easy — Serves 8 to 10

Rinse and drain the beans, peas and hominy and place in a large bowl. Add the tomatoes, two avocados, the onion, bell peppers and celery and mix gently. Combine the salad dressing, honey, mustard, salt and pepper in a bowl and blend until smooth. Pour over the vegetable mixture and mix gently. Cover and chill in the refrigerator until ready to serve.

To serve, garnish with one sliced avocado and serve with tortilla chips (Note: The salsa may be stored in the refrigerator for up to one week, but is best served the same day. You may also garnish with sour cream. The salsa may be served on crisp salad greens as a salad or as a side dish.)

1 (15-ounce) can black beans

1 (15-ounce) can white
    Northern beans

1 (15-ounce) can pinto beans

1 (15-ounce) can garbanzo beans
    or chickpeas

1 (15-ounce) can black-eyed peas

1 (15-ounce) can white hominy

1 (15-ounce) can yellow hominy or
    whole kernel yellow corn

2 tomatoes, chopped and drained

2 avocados, cut into small pieces

1 red onion, chopped

1/2 green bell pepper, chopped

1/2 red or yellow bell pepper, chopped

1 cup chopped celery

1 (16-ounce) bottle Italian
    salad dressing

3/4 cup honey, at room temperature

2 tablespoons yellow mustard

Salt and coarsely ground pepper
    to taste

1 avocado, sliced

Marinated Asparagus

Moderate — Serves 6 to 8

2/3 cup packed light brown sugar

2/3 cup cider vinegar

2/3 cup olive oil

2/3 cup soy sauce

4 teaspoons lemon juice

1 teaspoon garlic powder

2 pounds fresh asparagus, trimmed

1 cup chopped toasted pecans

Mix the brown sugar, vinegar, olive oil, soy sauce, lemon juice and garlic powder in a saucepan. Bring to a boil and then reduce the heat. Simmer for 5 minutes. Place the asparagus in 1/2 inch of water in a saucepan. Bring to a boil and then reduce the heat. Simmer for 3 to 5 minutes or until tender-crisp. Drain the asparagus and place in a large sealable plastic bag. Add the marinade and seal the bag, turning to coat the asparagus. Marinate in the refrigerator until ready to serve.

To serve, drain the asparagus, discarding the marinade. Place the asparagus in a serving bowl and sprinkle with the pecans.

In 2006 The Junior League of Annapolis, along with 225 Junior League chapters across four countries, participated in Junior Leagues' Kids in the Kitchen, a spotlight on healthy eating and the ill effects of obesity and poor nutrition. Collectively, the program reached over eighty million participants. Junior League Annapolis volunteers held their event for fourth and fifth graders at Marley Elementary school, where children made healthful snacks, played relay games relating to healthy foods, and received education and take-home materials on how to buy inexpensive yet healthful foods. To view the extensive collection of healthy recipes for kids, to take food quizzes and learn fun food facts, or to get more information on this program, visit http://kidsinthekitchen.ajli.org/.

Lemon Jell-O Cake

Easy — Serves 8 to 10

To prepare the glaze, combine the confectioner's sugar and lemon juice in a small bowl and mix until smooth.

To prepare the cake, dissolve the Jell-O mix in the boiling water in a small heatproof bowl. Let stand until slightly cool. Combine the cake mix and dissolved Jell-O in a mixing bowl. Add the eggs, oil and lemon extract and mix well. Pour into a greased and floured bundt or tube pan. Bake at 350 degrees for 30 to 60 minutes or until a wooden pick inserted in the center comes out clean. Cool in the pan for 10 minutes. Invert onto a serving plate. Spoon the glaze over the hot cake. (Note: For a thicker glaze as photographed, add an additional 1 cup confectioners' sugar to the glaze.

Photograph for this recipe appears on page 45.

Lemon Glaze

2 cups confectioner's sugar

Juice of 2 lemons

Cake

1 (3-ounce) package lemon
    Jell-O mix

1 cup boiling water

1 (2-layer) package yellow cake mix

4 eggs

3/4 cup vegetable oil

1 tablespoon lemon extract

Black-Eyed Susans

Easy — Serves 2

1 ounce vodka

1 ounce light rum

1/2 ounce Cointreau

6 ounces orange juice

3 ounces pineapple juice

Squeeze of fresh lime juice

2 pineapple slices

Combine the vodka, rum, Cointreau, orange juice, pineapple juice and lime juice in a cocktail shaker and shake to mix well. Pour over ice in two tall glasses and garnish each with a pineapple slice.

Quick-Rise Bread

Easy — Makes 2 loaves

4 to 5 cups all-purpose flour

2 envelopes dry yeast

2 tablespoons sugar

1 tablespoon salt

1/4 cup vegetable oil

2 1/4 cups warm water (130 degrees)

Melted butter for brushing

Mix 2 cups of the flour, the yeast, sugar and salt in a large bowl. Add the oil and one-half of the warm water and beat well. Stir in the remaining warm water and enough of the remaining flour to make a soft dough. Cover and let stand at room temperature for 20 minutes. Place the dough on a heavily floured surface and knead briefly. Divide the dough into two equal portions. Shape each portion into a loaf and place in oiled 5x8-inch loaf pans. Cover lightly and chill for 2 to 24 hours.

Remove the dough from the refrigerator and let the dough rise in a warm place for 1 hour or until doubled in bulk before baking. Brush the top of the loaves with melted butter. Bake at 325 to 350 degrees for 40 minutes or until the loaves test done.

Bacon and Double-Cheese Quiche

Moderate — Serves 4 to 6

To prepare the pastry, mix the flour and salt in a large bowl. Cut in the butter to form coarse crumbs using a pastry blender or 2 knives. Stir in the water 1 tablespoonful at a time to form a soft dough. Shape the dough into a disk and wrap in plastic wrap. Chill for 30 minutes. Roll the pastry into an 11-inch circle with a lightly floured rolling pin on a lightly floured surface. Fit into a 9-inch quiche dish or pie plate, trimming the edge. Prick the dough with a fork. Line with foil and fill with pie weights or dried beans. Bake at 375 degrees for 10 minutes. Remove the weights and foil. Bake for 5 minutes longer or until light golden brown. Cool on a wire rack. Maintain the oven temperature.

To prepare the quiche, whisk the eggs, cream, thyme and white pepper in a small bowl. Pour into the cooled crust. Sprinkle with the bacon, Gruyère cheese and Cheddar cheese. Bake for 30 minutes or until the custard is set. Serve warm. (Note: The baked quiche may be stored in the freezer for up to one month. You may use a purchased frozen pie pastry to save time.)

Butter Pastry

1 1/3 cups all-purpose flour

1/8 teaspoon salt

1/4 cup (1/2 stick) butter, chilled and
   cut into pieces

2 to 3 tablespoons cold water

Quiche Filling and Assembly

4 eggs

1 1/2 cups light cream

1/4 teaspoon dried thyme

1/8 teaspoon white pepper

12 slices lean bacon, crisp-cooked
   and crumbled

1/2 cup (2 ounces) shredded
   Gruyère cheese

1/2 cup (2 ounces) shredded white
   Cheddar cheese

Oriental Salad

Easy — Serves 6 to 8

1 bunch green onions, chopped

1 (16-ounce) package broccoli slaw
   or coleslaw mix

1 cup slivered almonds

1 cup sunflower seeds

2 (3-ounce) packages Oriental
   ramen noodles

1 cup sugar

1 cup canola oil

2/3 cup balsamic vinegar

Combine the green onions, broccoli slaw, almonds and sunflower seeds in a bowl and toss to mix. Break the ramen noodles into pieces. Cook the ramen noodles in a saucepan using the package directions, reserving the seasoning packets; drain. Heat the sugar and canola oil in a small saucepan, stirring constantly. Remove from the heat and cool for 30 minutes. Add the vinegar and reserved seasoning packets and mix well. Pour over the broccoli mixture. Add the ramen noodles and toss to mix. Chill, covered, in the refrigerator until ready to serve.

Charcoaled Beef Tenderloin

Easy — Serves 10 to 15

1/4 cup Worcestershire sauce

1/4 cup wine vinegar

1/2 cup A.1. steak sauce

1/4 cup packed brown sugar

2/3 cup ketchup

2 teaspoons MSG

Cayenne pepper to taste

1 (2- to 3-pound) beef tenderloin

Fresh mushroom caps

Sprigs of fresh parsley

Blend the Worcestershire sauce, vinegar, steak sauce, brown sugar, ketchup, MSG and cayenne pepper in a bowl. Place the beef on a sheet of heavy-duty foil. Pour the marinade over the beef and wrap in the foil to enclose. Marinate in the refrigerator for 8 to 10 hours.

Place the foil-wrapped beef on a grill rack. Grill, covered, over low coals and hickory chips to 145 degrees on a meat thermometer for medium-rare or 160 degrees on a meat thermometer for medium, unwrapping and basting with the marinade occasionally. Remove from the heat and let stand for 15 minutes. Unwrap and cut the beef into thin slices. Place on a platter and garnish with mushroom caps and parsley.

Salsa Couscous Chicken

Easy — Serves 8

Sauté the almonds in hot olive oil in a skillet for 1 to 2 minutes or until golden brown. Remove the almonds from the skillet and set aside. Add the garlic to the skillet and sauté for 30 seconds. Add the chicken and sauté for 4 to 5 minutes or until brown.

Combine the salsa, currants, honey, cumin and cinnamon in a bowl and mix well. Add to the chicken and reduce the heat to medium. Cover and cook for 20 minutes or until the chicken is cooked through. Stir in the almonds. Spoon over the couscous.

1/2 cup coarsely chopped almonds

2 tablespoons olive oil

4 garlic cloves, minced

8 chicken thighs or boneless skinless
    chicken thighs

2 cups salsa

1/4 cup dried currants

2 tablespoons honey

1 1/2 teaspoons cumin

1 teaspoon cinnamon

1 (10-ounce) package
    couscous, cooked and kept warm

Cashew Rice Pilaf

Easy — Serves 10 to 12

Heat the butter in a ovenproof skillet over low heat until melted. Add the rice, cashews, cinnamon and cloves and cook for 5 to 10 minutes, stirring constantly.

Bring the water and bouillon cubes to a boil in a saucepan, stirring occasionally. Add to the rice mixture and mix well. Bake at 350 degrees for 30 minutes or until most of the water is absorbed.

1/2 cup (1 stick) unsalted butter

3 cups rice

1 cup cashew pieces

1 1/2 teaspoons cinnamon

Ground cloves to taste

6 1/2 cups water

6 chicken bouillon cubes

Chocolate Toffee Cherry Cookies

Moderate — Makes 2 to 3 dozen

1 1/2 cups all-purpose flour

1 teaspoon baking soda

1 cup (2 sticks) margarine, softened

3/4 cup granulated sugar

3/4 cup light brown sugar

1 egg

1 teaspoon vanilla extract

1 1/2 cups rolled oats

1 cup miniature chocolate chips

8 ounces milk chocolate-covered
   toffee pieces

1 (5-ounce) package dried
   cherries, ground

Sift the flour and baking soda together. Cream the margarine, granulated sugar and brown sugar with a paddle attachment at medium-high speed in a mixing bowl for 2 to 3 minutes or until light and fluffy, scraping down the side of the bowl once or twice. Add the egg and beat at high speed until combined. Add the vanilla and mix well, scraping down the side of the bowl. Add the flour mixture gradually, beating at low speed until combined. Add the oats, chocolate chips and toffee pieces and mix well. Sprinkle the cherries over the dough and mix well.

Divide the dough into three equal portions. Roll each portion into a log 1 1/2 inches in diameter using plastic wrap. Chill, wrapped in plastic wrap, in the refrigerator. Cut the logs into slices 3/4 inch thick and place on cookie sheets lined with baking parchment. Bake at 350 degrees for 8 to 10 minutes or until golden brown. Remove to wire racks to cool. (Note: Instead of shaping the dough into logs, you may drop the dough by spoonfuls onto the cookie sheets.)

A Thyme to Entertain

French Fresh Fruit Flan

Gourmet — Serves 10 to 12

Process the almonds, butter, 1/2 cup sugar and the flour in a food processor until combined. Add the egg yolk, 1 teaspoon vanilla and 1/2 teaspoon almond extract and blend until the dough holds together. Press onto the bottom and up the side of an 11-inch tart pan with a removable bottom. Bake at 375 degrees for 15 minutes or until golden brown. Remove from the oven to cool.

Beat the cream cheese, 3 tablespoons sugar, 2 tablespoons amaretto, 1 teaspoon vanilla extract and 1/2 teaspoon almond extract in a mixing bowl until smooth. Spread evenly in the cooled crust. Chill for 30 minutes or until firm.

Combine the preserves, 2 tablespoons amaretto and the lemon juice in a small saucepan. Cook over low heat until hot. Strain through a fine sieve into a bowl, discarding the solids. Let stand until cool.

Use blueberries to make the outline of a star in the center of the tart. Fill the star shape with strawberries and raspberries. Fill the outer area of the star with bananas. Brush with the glaze. Let stand for 1 to 2 hours for the glaze to harden. Serve slightly chilled or at room temperature. (Note: Great to serve for a Fourth of July, Memorial Day or Labor Day party. The crust may be made up to one day ahead. The fruit also may be arranged in concentric circles on top.)

2/3 cup ground almonds

1/2 cup (1 stick) butter, softened

1/2 cup sugar

1 1/2 cups all-purpose flour

1 egg yolk

1 teaspoon vanilla extract

1/2 teaspoon almond extract

8 ounces light cream cheese softened

3 tablespoons sugar

2 tablespoons amaretto

1 teaspoon vanilla extract

1/2 teaspoon almond extract

1/2 cup apricot preserves or
    orange marmalade

2 tablespoons amaretto

1 tablespoon lemon juice

3 to 4 cups fresh fruit (blueberries,
    strawberry halves, raspberries
    and sliced bananas)

MALLETS
ON THE
lawn

The annual croquet match between St. John's College and the U.S. Naval Academy

began in 1983. This grand spring lawn party, held in late April, is also a highly

touted spectator sport, with up to two thousand attending. There are lavish picnics on

the grass, serenades by St. John's Freshman Chorus, and USNA Plebes serving drinks

on silver platters. Many of the female spectators are dressed in nineteenth-century

long dresses with parasols, and men are often in bowler hats and striped jackets.

Johnnies wear clothing that reflects the college's independent culture, while Mids don

spotless, crisp, white attire that represents the academy's uniformity.

Mallets on the Lawn

Cuban Mojito

White Chocolate Mousse Dip

Creamy Brie Soup

Lemon Garlic Shrimp

Broccoli Sauté à la Niçoise

Spicy Beef Tenderloin

Johnnies Chocolate Zucchini Cake

...a grand spring lawn party

Cuban Mojito

Moderate — Serves 4

1/3 cup sugar

1/2 cup fresh mint leaves,
    coarsely chopped

1/2 cup fresh lime juice

1 cup light rum

Seltzer water or club soda, chilled

4 sprigs of fresh mint

4 lime slices

Muddle the sugar, 1/2 cup mint and the lime juice in a large pitcher and chill for 8 to 10 hours. Strain the mixture and pour back into the pitcher. Stir in the rum. Divide the mixture evenly among four 10-ounce drinking glasses. Top off with crushed ice and seltzer water. Garnish each glass with a sprig of mint and a lime slice. (Note: The kitchen tool used to muddle is a small wooden baseball bat-like object called a muddler. A wooden spoon can be used if you do not have one.)

Photograph for this recipe appears on page 61.

White Chocolate Mousse Dip

Easy — Serves 10 to 12

8 ounces light whipped topping

1 (3-ounce) package white chocolate
    instant pudding mix

1/2 to 1 cup Kahlúa

Beat the whipped topping and the pudding mix in a mixing bowl until smooth. Add the liqueur gradually, mixing at low speed until incorporated. Increase the speed to medium and beat for 1 to 2 minutes or until the mixture thickens. Chill, covered, for 10 minutes. Serve with strawberries and green apples. (Note: Do not use fat-free whipped topping, it will be too runny, and do not use regular whipped topping, it will be too thick. For a variation, you may use cheesecake or coconut cream instant pudding mix instead of white chocolate.)

A Thyme to Entertain

Creamy Brie Soup

Easy — Serves 6 to 8

Sauté the onion and celery in the butter in a skillet until tender. Stir in the flour. Remove from the heat and whisk in the milk and broth. Return to the heat and bring to a simmer. Simmer until heated through. Add the cheese and cook until melted, stirring constantly. Season with salt and pepper. Process in a food processor until smooth and creamy. Spoon into serving bowls. Garnish with chopped chives and serve with apple slices.

1/2 cup chopped onion

1/2 cup sliced celery

1/4 cup (1/2 stick) butter, melted

1/4 cup all-purpose flour

2 cups milk

2 cups chicken broth

12 ounces Brie cheese (including rind), cut into cubes

Salt and pepper to taste

Chopped chives

Lemon Garlic Shrimp

Moderate — Serves 10

Arrange the shrimp in a shallow baking pan. Add the celery and garlic. Squeeze the juice from the lemons over the top, reserving the lemon rinds. Dot with the butter and sprinkle with the pepper, Worcestershire sauce and hot sauce. Arrange the lemons face down over the top. Place on the highest oven rack and broil for 5 minutes or until the butter begins to melt. Bake at 350 degrees for 20 to 30 minutes or until the shrimp turn pink, being careful not to overcook. Remove the celery and lemon rinds before serving. Serve with French bread for soaking up the sauce.

5 pounds unpeeled shrimp

1 bunch celery with leaves, ribs separated

3 or 4 garlic cloves, chopped

6 lemons, cut into halves

2 cups (4 sticks) butter

1/2 (1-ounce) jar cracked black pepper

1/4 cup Worcestershire sauce

Hot red pepper sauce to taste

Broccoli Sauté à la Niçoise

Moderate — Serves 4 to 6

2 pounds broccoli, trimmed

Salt to taste

3 slices bacon, chopped

1/2 cup bread crumbs

3 tablespoons vegetable oil

1/2 cup minced onion

1 garlic clove, minced

1/3 to 1/2 cup grated
   Parmesan cheese

Freshly ground pepper to taste

Blanch the broccoli in boiling salted water in a stockpot until tender; drain and set aside. Cook the bacon in a skillet until crisp. Drain the bacon and set aside, reserving the pan drippings in the skillet. Brown the bread crumbs in the reserved pan drippings. Remove the bread crumbs and set aside. Heat the oil in the skillet. Add the onion and garlic and sauté until translucent. Add the broccoli and toss to coat and heat through. Add the bread crumbs, bacon and cheese. Season with salt and pepper. Toss and serve immediately.

Spicy Beef Tenderloin

Easy — Serves 8 to 10

1 cup port

1 cup soy sauce

1/2 cup olive oil

1 teaspoon pepper

1 teaspoon dried thyme

1/2 teaspoon hot red pepper sauce

4 garlic cloves, crushed

1 bay leaf, crumbled

1 (5- to 6-pound) beef tenderloin

1/2 cup water

Whisk the port, soy sauce and olive oil in a bowl. Whisk in the pepper, thyme, hot sauce, garlic and bay leaf. Pour the mixture over the tenderloin in a shallow baking dish. Cover tightly and marinate in the refrigerator for 8 hours, turning occasionally. Drain the tenderloin, reserving the marinade. Strain the marinade into a bowl and set aside, discarding any solids. Place the tenderloin on a rack in a baking pan. Bake at 425 degrees for 55 to 60 minutes or until a meat thermometer registers 145 degrees for medium-rare or 160 degrees for medium. Combine the reserved marinade, pan drippings from the tenderloin and water in a saucepan and bring to a boil. Boil for 2 to 3 minutes, stirring constantly. Slice the tenderloin and serve with the sauce.

A Thyme to Entertain

Johnnies Chocolate Zucchini Cake

Moderate — Serves 15

Sift the flour, baking cocoa, baking soda, pudding mix and salt together; set aside. Cream the butter, oil and sugar in a mixing bowl until light and fluffy. Add the eggs one at a time, mixing well after each addition. Mix in the vanilla. Add the dry ingredients alternately with the buttermilk, mixing well after each addition. Stir in the zucchini. Pour the batter into a 9x13-inch cake pan. Sprinkle with the chocolate chips and walnuts. Bake at 325 degrees for 40 to 55 minutes or until the cake tests done.

$2^1/2$ cups all-purpose flour

$1^1/4$ cups baking cocoa

1 teaspoon baking soda

1 (3-ounce) package chocolate instant pudding mix

1 teaspoon salt

$1/2$ cup (1 stick) butter, softened

$1/2$ cup vegetable oil

$1^3/4$ cups sugar

3 eggs

1 teaspoon vanilla extract

$1/2$ cup buttermilk

2 cups grated zucchini

1 cup (6 ounces) chocolate chips

$3/4$ cup chopped walnuts

Girly Girl Cocktail

Easy — Makes a variable amount

Combine equal parts cranberry juice, Champagne and vodka in a martini pitcher and stir gently. Serve in martini glasses rimmed with sparkling pink sugar.

Cranberry juice, chilled

Champagne, chilled

Raspberry-flavored vodka, chilled

Sparkling pink sugar

Mids Caramel Apple Muffins

Easy — Makes 1 dozen

2 cups all-purpose flour

3/4 cup sugar

2 1/2 teaspoons cinnamon

2 teaspoons baking powder

1/2 teaspoon salt

1 cup milk

1 egg, lightly beaten

1/4 cup (1/2 stick) unsalted
    butter, melted

1 1/2 teaspoons vanilla extract

1/2 cup chopped peeled apples

3/4 cup chopped caramels
    (about 12)

Combine the flour, sugar, cinnamon, baking powder and salt in a bowl. Combine the milk and egg in a large bowl and mix well. Stir in the butter and vanilla. Add the dry ingredients and mix well. Stir in the apples and caramels. Divide the batter among twelve greased muffin cups. Bake at 350 degrees for 25 minutes or until the muffin tops spring back when lightly pressed. Serve immediately.

Broiled Pesto Tomato Halves

Easy — Serves 8

4 cups chopped fresh basil leaves

1/2 cup chopped parsley

1/2 cup olive oil

1/2 cup pine nuts

3 small garlic cloves, chopped

1/2 cup (2 ounces) grated
    Parmesan cheese

1 teaspoon salt

4 large firm tomatoes

1/4 cup dry bread crumbs

Process the basil, parsley, olive oil, pine nuts and garlic in a food processor until blended. Add the cheese and salt and process until smooth. Slice the tomatoes horizontally into halves and arrange cut side up on a baking sheet. Bake at 350 degrees for 5 to 10 minutes. Spread the top of each tomato with the pesto and lightly sprinkle with the bread crumbs. Place the baking sheet on the highest oven rack and broil for 2 minutes. Serve immediately. (Note: You may substitute 1 cup dried basil for the fresh basil leaves.)

White Chicken Chili

Easy — Serves 6

Sauté the onions and garlic in the hot olive oil in a 4-quart heavy saucepan until translucent. Stir in the ginger and oregano. Add the chicken broth, wine and bay leaf and mix well. Simmer for 10 minutes. Add the chicken, beans and jalapeño chile and mix well. Cook, uncovered, for 10 minutes. Stir in the cheese one handful at a time until melted. Remove the bay leaf just before serving. Serve with assorted toppings, such as sliced black olives, chopped avocado, shredded Cheddar cheese, chopped green onions, salsa and sour cream, on the side. (Note: You may substitute Great Northern beans for the cannellini.)

1 1/2 cups chopped onions

3 garlic cloves, minced

1 tablespoon olive oil

1/2 teaspoon dried ginger

2 teaspoons dried oregano

2 cups chicken broth

1/2 cup dry white wine

1 bay leaf

2 cups chopped cooked chicken
    breasts

1 (16-ounce) can cannellini

1 jalapeño chile, seeded and minced

1 1/2 cups (6 ounces) shredded
    Monterey Jack cheese

Latin Pork Tenderloin Salad

Easy — Serves 6

Citrus Vinaigrette

1/4 cup fresh lime juice

1/4 cup fresh orange juice

1/4 cup red wine vinegar

2 teaspoons sugar

1/3 cup coarsely chopped
    fresh oregano

1 teaspoon minced garlic

1/3 cup olive oil

Salad and Assembly

1 (20-ounce) pork tenderloin

Mixed salad greens

2 large tomatoes, chopped

2 avocados, chopped

1 or 2 (15-ounce) cans black
    beans, drained

1 or 2 (8-ounce) cans whole kernel
    corn, drained

1 red onion, chopped

To prepare the vinaigrette, whisk the lime juice, orange juice, vinegar and sugar in a bowl until the sugar is dissolved. Whisk in the oregano and garlic. Add the olive oil gradually, whisking constantly until incorporated.

To prepare the salad, place the pork on a grill rack and grill over medium-low heat until a meat thermometer inserted into the thickest portion registers 160 to 170 degrees. Remove from the grill and let rest for 5 to 10 minutes. Cut the pork into slices.

To serve, arrange salad greens on six salad plates. Top with the tomatoes, avocadoes, black beans, corn and onion. Drizzle with the vinaigrette and top with the warm pork. (Note: You may use sliced grape tomatoes instead of the large tomatoes. Teriyaki-marinated pork tenderloin may also be used.)

A Thyme to Entertain

Mexican Lasagna

Moderate — Serves 4 to 6

Cook the chicken in boiling water in a stockpot until cooked through. Drain the chicken, discarding the liquid. Let stand until completely cool. Shred the chicken using a fork. Combine the soup and tomatoes in a bowl and mix well. Stir in the jalapeño chiles and season with salt and pepper. Reserve some of the soup mixture and some of the cheese. Layer tortillas, the chicken, remaining soup mixture and remaining cheese alternately in a buttered 2-quart round baking dish until all of the ingredients are used, ending with a tortilla. Top with the reserved soup mixture and cheese. Bake, covered, at 350 degrees for 20 minutes. Bake, uncovered, for 10 minutes longer. Serve immediately.

4 to 6 boneless skinless
   chicken breasts
2 (10-ounce) cans cream of
   chicken soup
1 (14-ounce) can Mexican tomatoes,
   or 1 large jar salsa
1 (4-ounce) can jalapeño chiles,
   chopped, or to taste
Salt and pepper to taste
4 cups (16 ounces) shredded Mexican
   blend cheese
Large flour tortillas

The annual St. John's College versus the U.S. Naval Academy croquet match is also known as the Annapolis Cup. It has been a festive spring event for over twenty-four years and started as a challenge by the commandant of the Naval Academy to a St. John's freshman to find an athletic contest that the Johnnies could win. St. John's proposed a croquet match, and the rest is history.

Champion Lemon Squares

Easy — Makes 3 dozen

Crust

1 cup (2 sticks) butter, softened

1/2 cup sugar

2 cups all-purpose flour

Filling

1 3/4 cups sugar

4 eggs, lightly beaten

6 tablespoons lemon juice

2 teaspoons grated lemon zest
   (optional)

3 tablespoons all-purpose flour

To prepare the crust, cream the butter and sugar in a mixing bowl until light and fluffy. Blend in the flour. Press in the bottom of a 9x13-inch baking dish. Bake at 350 degrees for 20 minutes.

To prepare the filling, blend the sugar and eggs in a bowl until smooth. Stir in the lemon juice, lemon zest and flour. Pour the filling over the crust and bake for 20 to 25 minutes or until the filling is set.

The Teen Resource Guide, a Junior League of Annapolis, Inc. publication, is a guide provided to assist Anne Arundel County teenagers in coping with issues that may arise during their teenage years. The guide includes an introduction to services that are available free of charge in the county as well as phone numbers for various crisis hotlines and agencies providing assistance and guidance. Referral phone numbers and Web addresses are given for many areas of concern. The Teen Resource Guide has served as a valuable tool to guidance counselors, school nurses, police officers, educators, and many others who deal with the struggles facing our teenage population. The demand for the guide has stayed strong since it was first published in 1992, and it has become an integral part of the resources used by those who support our children.

A Thyme to Entertain

Triple-Decker Key Lime Pie

Moderate — Serves 8

To prepare the crust, pulse the granola in a food processor until slightly ground. Combine the granola, graham cracker crumbs, butter and sugar in a bowl and mix well. Press into a 9-inch pie plate. Bake at 350 degrees for 10 minutes. Remove from the oven and let stand until completely cool.

To prepare the pie, whisk 14 ounces sweetened condensed milk, 1/2 cup Key Lime juice and the egg yolks in a bowl until smooth. Pour evenly over the crust and bake at 300 degrees for 25 minutes. Remove from the oven and let stand until completely cool. Beat the cream cheese, 1/2 cup sweetened condensed milk, 1/4 cup Key lime juice, the sugar and vanilla in a mixing bowl until smooth. Pour over the baked layer. Chill, covered, for 4 to 10 hours. Spread sweetened whipped cream over the top of the pie just before serving. Garnish with lime slices.

Crust

3/4 cup plain granola

3/4 cup graham cracker crumbs

1/4 cup (1/2 stick) butter, melted

3 tablespoons sugar

Pie

1 (14-ounce) can sweetened
　　condensed milk

1/2 cup Key lime juice

3 egg yolks

8 ounces cream cheese, softened

1/2 cup sweetened condensed milk

1/4 cup Key lime juice

2 tablespoons sugar

1 teaspoon vanilla extract

Sweetened whipped cream, or frozen
　　whipped topping, thawed

Lime slices

SPRING IS IN THE AIR!

As tulips and daffodils begin to stretch their green petals, Annapolis comes alive with energy and excitement. Awakening from the cold winter, Annapolitans bustle down the cobblestone streets to the City Dock and visit the Market House for morning bagels and coffee. They shop on Main Street for fashions and meet for evening drinks and seafood under the spring moonlight.

Annual events, including the May Day Basket Contest and Bay Bridge Walk, kick off the season, followed by the opening of the Annapolis Summer Garden Theatre. This outdoor theatre at the City Dock holds performances during the summer months only.

Spring Is in the Air!

Overnight Artichoke and Ham Strata

Jalapeño Cheese Squares

Sweet Vegetable Dip

Margarita Shrimp Salad

Cilantro Chicken Sandwiches

Strawberry Shortcake
with
Whipped Almond Frosting

...as tulips and daffodils begin to stretch

Overnight Artichoke and Ham Strata

Easy — Serves 6

1 (14-ounce) can artichoke hearts

3 English muffins, split and quartered

2 tablespoons butter, melted

1 cup chopped lean ham

1/2 cup (2 ounces) grated fresh
    Parmesan cheese

2 tablespoons chopped fresh chives

2 large garlic cloves, minced

1 (12-ounce) can evaporated
    fat-free milk

3 eggs

3 egg whites

1/8 teaspoon ground nutmeg

Large sprig of fresh parsley

Drain and chop the artichoke hearts. Place the muffin quarters crust side down in an 8x8-inch baking dish coated with nonstick cooking spray. Drizzle with the butter. Layer the ham, cheese, artichoke hearts, chives and garlic over the muffin quarters. Whisk the evaporated milk, eggs, egg whites and nutmeg in a bowl and pour over the layers. Chill, covered, for 8 to 10 hours.

Uncover the strata and bake at 375 degrees for 50 minutes or until set. Let stand for 10 minutes before serving. Garnish the center with a large sprig of fresh parsley. (Note: Do not use marinated artichoke hearts in this recipe.)

In downtown Annapolis on May 1st, spring flowers overflow from baskets hung from doors and placed on porches. A tradition for over fifty years in the city, residents and retailers place beautiful fresh-cut flower baskets throughout the city to celebrate the arrival of spring. The Garden Club of Old Annapolis organizes a walking tour to see all of the floral bounty and a May basket competition.

A Thyme to Entertain

Jalapeño Cheese Squares

Easy — Serves 10 to 12

Chop and drain the tomato. Spread 1/2 cup of the green chiles evenly in a lightly buttered 9x13-inch baking dish. Add the Cheddar cheese and Monterey Jack cheese and press firmly to form a crust. Sprinkle with the salt, Worcestershire sauce and garlic powder. Spread the remaining 1/4 cup green chiles, onion and tomato over the layers. Pour the eggs over the top. Bake at 300 degrees for 25 to 30 minutes or until partially set. Turn off the oven and open the oven door. Let stand in the oven for 10 minutes. Sprinkle with hot sauce.

1 small fresh tomato

3/4 cup canned diced jalapeño chiles

12 ounces each Cheddar cheese and
   Monterey Jack cheese, shredded

1/4 teaspoon salt

Dash of Worcestershire sauce

Pinch of garlic powder

1/4 cup chopped Vidalia onion

12 eggs, beaten

Hot red pepper sauce to taste

Sweet Vegetable Dip

Easy — Serves 10 to 15

Combine the peas, corn, bell pepper, onion and pimento in a bowl and stir to mix well. Mix the sugar, vinegar, oil and teriyaki sauce in a small bowl. Pour over the vegetable mixture and stir to mix. Marinate, covered, in the refrigerator for several hours. To serve, drain the vegetable mixture, discarding the marinade. Serve with tortilla chips.

1 (15-ounce) can black-eyed
   peas, drained

1 (11-ounce) can Shoe Peg
   corn, drained

1 large green bell pepper, chopped

1 onion, chopped

1 (4-ounce) jar chopped
   pimento, drained

3/4 cup sugar

1/2 cup cider vinegar

1/2 cup vegetable oil

1 tablespoon teriyaki sauce

Margarita Shrimp Salad

Gourmet — Serves 4 to 6

Avocado Vinaigrette

1 1/4 cups light olive oil

1/2 cup white wine vinegar

1/4 cup lime juice

1/4 cup cilantro leaves

1/2 teaspoon salt

1/8 teaspoon cayenne pepper

1 avocado, coarsely chopped

Salad

1 cup canned black beans

1 cup lime juice

1/2 cup white tequila

2 tablespoons Triple Sec

1 tablespoon red pepper flakes

1 teaspoon kosher salt

1 pound (10- to 16-count) shrimp,
     peeled and deveined

1 cup each chopped roasted red and
     yellow bell pepper

1 cup roasted corn kernels

1 cup tomato, seeded and chopped

2/3 cup thinly sliced red onion

1/4 cup chopped cilantro leaves

1 tablespoon minced seeded
     jalapeño chile

Lime juice for dipping

Finely chopped cilantro

Baked tortilla strips

Lime slices

Chopped cilantro

To prepare the vinaigrette, process the olive oil, vinegar, lime juice, cilantro, salt and cayenne pepper in a food processor until blended. Add the avocado and pulse just until blended. (Do not overprocess or the mixture will become oily.) Store in the refrigerator.

To prepare the salad, rinse and drain the black beans. Combine 1/2 cup lime juice, the tequila, Triple Sec, red pepper flakes and kosher salt in a bowl and mix well. Add the shrimp. Marinate in the refrigerator for 30 minutes. Combine the black beans, bell peppers, corn, tomato, onion, 1/4 cup chopped cilantro and the jalapeño chile in a bowl and mix well. Drain the shrimp, discarding the marinade. Place the shrimp on a grill rack and grill until the shrimp turn pink. Add the hot shrimp to the vegetable mixture. Add 1/2 cup of the vinaigrette and toss to mix.

To serve, dip the rims of four to six margarita glasses in additional lime juice and then in finely chopped cilantro. Spoon the salad into the prepared glasses and garnish with baked tortilla strips, lime slices and chopped cilantro.

Photograph for this recipe appears on page 75.

A Thyme to Entertain

Cilantro Chicken Sandwiches

Easy — Serves 4

To prepare the dressing, process the cilantro, olive oil and kosher salt in a food processor until smooth.

To prepare the sandwiches, drizzle each side of the bread halves with a small amount of the cilantro dressing. Layer the sliced tomatoes, chicken and vegetables on the bottom half of the bread. Top with the remaining half of the bread and cut into four equal portions.

Cilantro Dressing

1/2 cup fresh cilantro leaves

5 tablespoons olive oil

1/4 teaspoon kosher salt

Sandwiches

1 long loaf fresh French bread,
    cut into halves lengthwise

2 large tomatoes, sliced

4 chicken breasts, grilled

2 cups grilled chopped vegetables
    (such as onions, mushrooms
    and squash)

Visit Historic London Town & Gardens. London Town is a beautiful park on the South River in Edgewater, Maryland. It began as a colonial seaport town founded in 1683 and is currently being excavated by archaeologists. It features a woodland garden and a native garden as well as the National Historic Landmark William Brown House.

Strawberry Shortcake with Whipped Almond Frosting

Moderate — Serves 8

Shortcake

2 cups all-purpose flour

2 teaspoons baking powder

1/2 cup sugar

1/2 cup (1 stick) butter, melted

2/3 cup milk

Whipped Almond Frosting

1/4 cup all-purpose flour

1 cup milk

1/2 cup (1 stick) butter, softened

1/2 cup shortening

1 cup sugar

1 teaspoon almond extract

Assembly

Sliced fresh strawberries

Sprigs of fresh mint

To prepare the shortcake, sift the flour and baking powder together into a bowl. Add the sugar and mix well. Blend in the butter. Stir in the milk. (The mixture will not be smooth.) Spoon the batter into a greased 9-inch or 8x8-inch cake pan. Bake at 450 degrees for 15 to 20 minutes or until the cake tests done. Cool in the pan for a few minutes. Invert onto a wire rack to cool completely.

To prepare the frosting, mix the flour and milk in a saucepan. Cook until thickened, stirring constantly. Remove from the heat and let stand until cool. Beat the butter, shortening and sugar in a mixing bowl until smooth. Beat in the almond extract. Add the cooled flour mixture and whip for 4 minutes.

To assemble, cut the cake horizontally into halves. Place the bottom layer cut side up on a cake plate. Spread 1 cup of the frosting over the layer and arrange sliced strawberries over the frosting. Top with the remaining layer cut side down. Cover the top with 1 cup of the remaining frosting and arrange sliced strawberries over the top. Place a large dollop of the remaining frosting in the center. Garnish with sprigs of fresh mint. Store in the refrigerator.

Frozen Peach Coladas

Easy — Serves 1 or 2

Blend the ice, rum, cream of coconut, peaches and ice cream in a blender until thick, adding additional ice cream if needed. Pour into serving glasses.

1/2 cup ice

2 ounces light rum

2 tablespoons cream of coconut

1 cup fresh or canned peaches

1 tablespoon (or more) vanilla
    ice cream

Fiesta Dip

Easy — Serves 6 to 8

Cut the uncooked corn from the cobs into a small bowl. Stir in the taco seasoning. Spread the cream cheese in an 8-inch pie plate or a rectangular dish that is only 2 to 3 inches deep. Drain the salsa in a colander, pressing out the liquid. Spread over the cream cheese. Layer the black beans and corn mixture over the salsa layer. Arrange the tomato in a 1-inch circle around the edge of the dish. (If you are using a rectangular dish, arrange the tomatoes in a 1- to 2-inch strip at each end of the dish.) Sprinkle the top with the chives. Chill, covered, for up to 24 hours before serving. Let stand at room temperature for 15 minutes before serving. Serve with tortilla chips.

3 ears fresh corn

2 tablespoons taco seasoning

8 ounces 1/3-less-fat cream
    cheese, softened

1 (16-ounce) jar chunky salsa
    (or more)

1 (16-ounce) can black beans,
    rinsed and drained

1 tomato, chopped

2 tablespoons (about) chopped
    fresh chives

Greek Tabouli Salad

Moderate — Serves 4 to 6

Yogurt Dressing

3 tablespoons olive oil

1 tablespoon vinegar

2 garlic cloves, chopped

1 teaspoon salt

1/4 teaspoon pepper

1 cup yogurt

1 cup sour cream

1/4 teaspoon dill weed

2 tablespoons grated
    Parmesan cheese

Salad

1 (5-ounce) package tabouli
    salad mix

1 (15-ounce) can garbanzo beans

1/2 cup finely chopped tomato

1/4 cup finely chopped green onions

1/4 cup finely chopped parsley

1 tablespoon lemon juice

Torn lettuce or mixed salad greens

1 tomato, cut into wedges

1 cucumber, sliced

4 ounces crumbled feta cheese

To prepare the dressing, combine the olive oil, vinegar, garlic, salt and pepper in a bowl and mix well. Add the yogurt, sour cream, dill weed and cheese and mix well. Chill, covered, in the refrigerator.

To prepare the salad, prepare the tabouli using the package directions. Let stand for 30 minutes. Add the beans, 1/2 cup chopped tomato, the green onions, parsley and lemon juice and mix well. Divide the lettuce among four to six salad plates. Place a scoop of the tabouli mixture on each. Top each with the tomato wedges and cucumber slices. Sprinkle with the feta cheese. Spoon the yogurt dressing over the top of each.

A Thyme to Entertain

Curried Chicken Salad

Moderate — Serves 4

Place the chicken and onion in a deep skillet and add enough water to cover the chicken. Bring to a boil and remove from the heat. Cover immediately and let stand for 20 minutes or until the chicken is cooked through. Remove the chicken to a plate and cool.

Chop the chutney and celery. Cut the mango and apple into 1/2-inch pieces. Combine the chutney, celery, mango, apple, yogurt, mayonnaise, raisins, curry powder, ginger and salt in a large bowl and mix well. Cut the cooled chicken into 1/2-inch pieces. Add the chicken to the fruit mixture and toss to coat. Serve on lettuce leaves or stuffed into tomato shells.

4 skinless boneless chicken breasts (about 1 pound)

1 onion, cut into quarters

1/4 cup mango chutney

2 ribs celery

1 large mango

1 Granny Smith apple

1/3 cup plain nonfat yogurt

1/4 cup mayonnaise

2 tablespoons golden raisins

2 teaspoons curry powder

1 1/2 teaspoons grated peeled ginger

1/4 teaspoon salt

Italian Tortellini Soup

Moderate — Serves 8

1 pound mild Italian sausage,
　　casings removed and
　　sausage sliced
1 cup chopped onion
2 large garlic cloves, chopped
6 cups beef stock
1/2 cup dry red cooking wine
1 (14-ounce) can chopped tomatoes
1 (15-ounce) can tomato sauce
2 large carrots, peeled and sliced
1 zucchini, chopped
1 green bell pepper, chopped
2 teaspoons Italian seasoning
1 (16-ounce) package frozen
　　cheese tortellini

Brown the sausage in a skillet. Remove the sausage from the skillet and set aside. Drain the drippings from the skillet. Sauté the onion and garlic in the skillet for 5 minutes. Combine the sausage, onion mixture, stock, wine, tomatoes, tomato sauce, carrots, zucchini, bell pepper and Italian seasoning in a large stockpot. Simmer for 30 minutes or until the vegetables are tender. Add the pasta and cook for 7 minutes or until tender. Ladle into soup bowls and sprinkle with cheese.

A Thyme to Entertain

Greek-Style Leg of Lamb

Easy — Serves 6 to 8

Combine the olive oil, vinegar, bay leaves, oregano, mint, thyme, garlic powder, salt and pepper in a bowl and mix well. Place the lamb in a sealable plastic bag. Add the marinade and seal the bag. Marinate in the refrigerator for 48 hours, turning occasionally. Drain the lamb, discarding the marinade.

Place the lamb on a grill rack. Grill, covered with the grill lid, over medium heat for 50 to 60 minutes or until 145 degrees on a meat thermometer for medium-rare, 160 degrees on a meat thermometer for medium or 170 degrees on a meat thermometer for well.

1 cup olive oil

1 cup white vinegar

6 bay leaves

1 tablespoon oregano

1 tablespoon dried mint, or 6 fresh
    mint leaves

1 teaspoon thyme

1 teaspoon garlic powder, or
    4 garlic cloves, crushed

2 teaspoons salt

1 1/2 teaspoons pepper

1 leg of lamb

Take time to visit the William Paca House and Gardens, a National Historic Landmark which was lovingly restored to its eighteenth-century colonial-era splendor by the Historic Annapolis Foundation. It was the home of William Paca, one of Maryland's four signers of the Declaration of Independence. The two-acre gardens have also been restored to their original multi-tier terrace design and are filled with plants known from the eighteenth century.

Mandarin Almond Chicken

Moderate — Serves 6

1/2 cup all-purpose flour

1/2 teaspoon salt

6 boneless whole chicken breasts

1/2 cup (1 stick) butter, melted

1 cup orange juice

1/4 cup cooking sherry

1/4 cup packed brown sugar

1/4 cup honey

2 tablespoons lemon juice

1 tablespoon soy sauce

1 tablespoon cornstarch

1/4 teaspoon ground ginger

1 (11-ounce) can mandarin
   oranges, drained

1/2 cup sliced almonds

1 tablespoon butter

Salt to taste

1 tablespoon chopped fresh parsley

Mix the flour and 1/2 teaspoon salt in a shallow dish. Add the chicken, turning to coat. Brush a small amount of the melted butter on the bottom of a 10x15-inch glass baking dish. Arrange the chicken in a single layer in the prepared dish. Pour the remaining melted butter over the chicken. Bake, uncovered, at 350 degrees for 1 hour.

Combine the orange juice, sherry, brown sugar, honey, lemon juice, soy sauce, cornstarch and ginger in a small saucepan and mix well. Bring to a boil over medium heat. Cook until smooth and thickened, stirring constantly. Spoon the sauce over the chicken and top with the mandarin oranges. Bake for 15 minutes. Sauté the almonds in 1 tablespoon butter in a skillet until light brown. Drain the almonds and season with salt. Remove the chicken from the oven and sprinkle with the almonds and parsley.

A Thyme to Entertain

Pineapple Cobbler

Easy — Serves 6 to 8

Combine the butter, sugar and eggs in a bowl and mix well. Fold in the pineapple and bread cubes. Spoon into a buttered 1¹/₂-quart baking dish. Bake at 350 degrees for 30 minutes. Remove from the oven and let stand for 10 to 15 minutes before serving. (Note: This recipe may be prepared ahead and chilled until ready to bake. This is great with ham for Easter or Christmas.)

1 cup (2 sticks) butter, melted

1¹/₂ cups sugar

3 eggs

1 (20-ounce) can pineapple chunks, drained

4 cups trimmed bread cubes

Miniature Éclairs

Easy — Serves 4 to 6

Beat the cream in a mixing bowl until foamy. Add the confectioners' sugar gradually, beating until soft peaks form. Stir in the Kahlúa. Spread over the bottom half of each ladyfinger and replace the tops. Spread each with 2 teaspoons of the fudge. Garnish with chocolate-covered coffee beans.

2/3 cup heavy whipping cream

2 tablespoons confectioners' sugar

2 tablespoons Kahlúa

1 (3-ounce) package ladyfingers, split into halves

¹/₂ cup purchased fudge sauce

Chocolate-covered coffee beans

BRIDGE
TO SHORE

The Chesapeake Bay Bridge Walk has attracted 60,000 people who want an opportunity to cross the bridge on foot. With a length of 4.3 miles, the William Preston Lane Jr. Memorial (Bay) Bridge is among the world's longest and most scenic overwater structures. It provides a direct connection between Maryland's Eastern Shore recreational and ocean regions and the metropolitan areas of Baltimore, Annapolis, and Washington, D.C. Traditionally held on the first Sunday in May, there is no better way to top off the Bridge Walk than to have all your friends join you back at your house for an afternoon of treats.

Bridge to Shore

Peach Perfection

Mediterranean Frittata

Hash Brown Casserole

St. Michael's Fruit Delight

Pound Cake

Coffee Crumble

...an afternoon of treats

Peach Perfection

Easy — Serves 6 to 8

1 (750-milliliter) bottle
    Champagne, chilled
2 cups white cranberry peach
    juice, chilled
1 cup peach schnapps, chilled
Whole strawberries
Fresh mint leaves

Combine the Champagne, white cranberry peach juice and schnapps in a punch bowl and stir gently to mix well. Add ice. Ladle into punch cups and garnish each serving with a strawberry or mint leaf.

Mediterranean Frittata

Moderate — Serves 6 to 8

Vegetables and Pasta

4 to 6 green onions
Olive oil for sautéing
1 large zucchini, or 2 small zucchini
1 (10-ounce) package frozen
    spinach, thawed
1 red bell pepper, roasted
    and chopped
1/2 cup chopped Greek olives
4 ounces Polish ham, rolled and
    sliced (about 3/4 cup)
4 ounces Genoa salami, julienned
    (about 3/4 cup)
2 cups cooked thin spaghetti or
    angel hair pasta

To prepare the vegetables and pasta, coarsely chop the green onions and sauté in olive oil in a skillet until tender. Cool to room temperature. Thinly slice the zucchini and sauté in olive oil in a skillet until brown. Cool to room temperature. Squeeze the spinach dry and sauté in olive oil in a skillet until heated through. Cool to room temperature. (Make sure all of the ingredients are at room temperature or warm before continuing with the recipe.) Combine the green onions, zucchini, spinach, bell pepper, olives, ham and salami in a large bowl and stir to mix well. Add the pasta and toss until all of the ingredients are evenly distributed.

To prepare the frittata, whisk the eggs, cream, oregano, salt and pepper in a large bowl. Stir in the feta cheese and 1/4 cup Parmesan cheese. Heat a 15-inch cast-iron skillet or large heavy ovenproof skillet until hot. Brush the bottom of the hot skillet with olive oil. Spread the pasta mixture evenly in the hot prepared skillet. Pour the egg mixture over the top and prod the mixture with a fork so the egg mixture penetrates to the bottom of the skillet. Cook over medium heat until the mixture begins to set. Arrange the tomatoes over the top and sprinkle with additional Parmesan cheese. Bake at 350 degrees for 15 to 20 minutes or until set and the top is bubbly and crusty. Remove from the oven and let stand for 10 minutes.

To prepare the sauce, combine the cucumber, sour cream, vinegar, garlic powder, salt and pepper in a bowl and mix well.

To serve, cut the frittata into wedges or into circles using a biscuit cutter and serve with the sauce.

Photograph for this recipe appears on page 91.

Frittata

18 eggs

1/4 cup heavy cream

1/2 teaspoon oregano

Salt and pepper to taste

3/4 to 1 cup crumbled feta cheese

1/4 to 1/2 cup (1 to 2 ounces) grated
    Parmesan cheese

Sliced tomatoes

Grated Parmesan cheese

Tzatziki Sauce

1 cucumber, peeled and grated

1/2 cup sour cream

2 tablespoons white vinegar

Garlic powder to taste

Salt and pepper to taste

Did you know that St. Michael's is referred to as the town that fooled the British? On the morning of August 10, 1813, residents of St. Michael's, having been forewarned of a British attack, hoisted lanterns to the masts of ships and in the tops of the trees. The height of light caused the British to overshoot the town. This first-known blackout was effective. Only one house was struck, and it is now known as the "Cannonball House."

Hash Brown Casserole

Easy — Serves 6 to 8

2 cups sour cream

1 (10-ounce) can cream of
celery soup

1/4 cup chopped onion

2 tablespoons dried minced garlic

Salt and pepper to taste

1 (2-pound) package shredded hash
brown potatoes

2 cups (8 ounces) shredded
Cheddar cheese

1 1/2 cups honey oat cereal, crumbled

1/4 cup (1/2 stick) butter, melted

Mix the sour cream, soup, onion, garlic, salt and pepper in a large bowl. Stir in the potatoes and cheese. Spoon into a buttered 9x13-inch baking dish. Sprinkle with the cereal and drizzle with the butter. Bake at 350 degrees for 40 to 50 minutes or until heated through.

St. Michael's Fruit Delight

Easy — Serves 10 to 12

1 1/3 cups pitted dried plums

1 1/3 cups dried apricots

1 1/3 cups undrained canned
pineapple chunks

1 (21-ounce) can sweetened
cherry pie filling

1/4 cup dry white wine

2 cups water

Layer the plums, apricots and pineapple in a greased 8x8-inch baking dish. Mix the pie filling, wine and water in a bowl. Pour over the fruit. Bake, covered, at 350 degrees for 1 1/4 hours. Uncover and bake for 15 minutes longer or until the top is lightly caramelized. Serve with pancakes, waffles, French toast, crepes or pound cake.

A Thyme to Entertain

Pound Cake

Moderate — Serves 12

Butter and flour a nonstick tube pan. Mix the cake flour, baking powder and salt together. Cream the butter and sugar in a mixing bowl until light and fluffy. Add the eggs one at a time, beating well after each addition. Add the flour mixture and milk alternately, beating well after each addition. Beat in the vanilla. Pour into the prepared pan. Bake at 325 degrees for 1 to 1 1/2 hours or until a wooden pick inserted in the center comes out clean. (Do not open the oven door too early—the cake will fall.) Cool in the pan for about 10 minutes. Invert onto a serving plate.

3 cups cake flour

1 teaspoon baking powder

1/2 teaspoon salt

1 cup (2 sticks) unsalted butter, softened

3 cups sugar

6 eggs

2/3 cup milk

1 teaspoon vanilla extract

Coffee Crumble

Easy — Serves 6 to 8

Mix the flour, baking powder, baking soda and 1/2 teaspoon cinnamon together. Cream the butter, granulated sugar and 1/4 cup brown sugar in a mixing bowl until light and fluffy. Beat in the egg. Add the flour mixture and buttermilk alternately, beating well after each addition. Spread the batter in a greased 8x8-inch baking pan. Mix 1/4 cup brown sugar, the pecans, 1/4 teaspoon cinnamon and the nutmeg in a bowl. Sprinkle over the batter. (At this point, you may cover and chill for 8 to 10 hours before baking.) Bake, uncovered, at 350 degrees for 30 to 45 minutes or until the coffee cake tests done. (Note: This recipe may be doubled and baked in an 8x11-inch baking pan.)

1 cup all-purpose flour

1/2 teaspoon baking powder

1/4 teaspoon baking soda

1/2 teaspoon cinnamon

1/3 cup butter or margarine, softened

1/2 cup granulated sugar

1/4 cup packed light brown sugar

1 egg, beaten

1/2 cup buttermilk

1/4 cup packed light brown sugar

1/4 cup chopped pecans

1/4 teaspoon cinnamon

1/8 teaspoon nutmeg

Cannonball Crab Soufflé

Moderate — Serves 8 to 10

1 pound crab meat

1 onion, finely chopped

1/2 cup finely chopped green
    bell pepper

4 green onions, chopped

8 ounces sliced mushrooms

1/4 cup (1/2 stick) butter, melted

14 slices white bread, crusts trimmed

8 ounces Monterey Jack
    cheese, shredded

8 ounces Cheddar cheese, shredded

12 eggs

1/4 cup milk

2 tablespoons white wine

1 teaspoon Worcestershire sauce

Hot red pepper sauce to taste

Salt and pepper to taste

Flake the crab meat, removing any shells. Sauté the onion, bell pepper, green onions and mushrooms in the butter in a skillet until tender-crisp. Line the bottom of a 3-quart baking dish with the bread. Layer the sautéed vegetables, Monterey Jack cheese, Cheddar cheese and crab meat over the bread. Beat the eggs, milk, wine, Worcestershire sauce, hot sauce, salt and pepper in a bowl. Pour over the layers. Cover and chill for 8 to 10 hours. Bake at 325 degrees for 1 hour.

Layered Cobb Salad

Easy — Serves 4 to 6

6 slices applewood smoked bacon

1 (12-ounce) package Bibb lettuce

2 yellow bell peppers

4 ounces provolone cheese, sliced

4 ounces roasted turkey, sliced

2 tomatoes, sliced

1 cup blue cheese vinaigrette

Cook the bacon in a skillet until crisp; drain and crumble. Tear the lettuce into bite-size pieces. Cut the bell peppers into bite-size pieces. Layer the lettuce, cheese, turkey, tomatoes, bell peppers and bacon in a large salad bowl. Pour the vinaigrette over the top just before serving. (Note: You may substitute roasted chicken for the turkey.)

Marinated Steak and Mushroom Salad

Easy — Serves 4

Cut the mushrooms into thin slices. Combine the oil, vinegar, soy sauce, parsley, green onions, salt and pepper in a large bowl and mix well. Add the steak and mushrooms and toss to coat. Marinate, covered, in the refrigerator for 2 to 24 hours. Serve over the salad greens.

8 ounces portobello mushrooms

1/4 cup vegetable oil

3 tablespoons cider vinegar

1 tablespoon soy sauce

1/4 cup minced fresh parsley

2 green onions, minced

1/2 teaspoon each salt and pepper

1 to 2 cups thinly sliced grilled
   sirloin steak

4 cups torn salad greens

Gourmet Macaroni and Cheese

Gourmet — Serves 8

Sauté the mushrooms and shallots in the butter in a skillet over medium-low heat. Cook, covered, for 10 minutes or until the shallots soften and most of the mushroom liquid cooks off. Process in a food processor to form a coarse paste. Add half the Parmesan cheese and mascarpone cheese and pulse to blend. Season with salt and pepper. Place in a pastry bag fitted with a plain tip. Butter the bottom and side of a heavy oval gratin dish. Layer the ham, fontina cheese and parsley in the prepared dish. Pipe the mushroom mixture into the rigatoni and layer in rows over the layers. Season the whipped cream with salt and pepper. Spread over the rigatoni. Sprinkle with the remaining Parmesan cheese. Bake at 375 degrees for 40 minutes or until the rigatoni is heated through. Broil for 2 minutes or until the top is brown.

4 cups chopped white mushrooms

1/2 cup chopped shallots

2 tablespoons unsalted butter, melted

1/2 cup (2 ounces) grated
   Parmesan cheese

1/4 cup mascarpone cheese

Salt and freshly ground pepper to taste

1 1/2 cups finely chopped boiled ham

1/2 cup finely chopped fontina cheese

1/2 cup flat-leaf parsley

3 to 4 cups cooked rigatoni, drained
   and chilled in ice water

1 1/2 cups heavy whipping
   cream, whipped

Grilled Pesto Chicken Breasts

Easy — Serves 12

Pesto

1 small garlic clove

1/4 cup pine nuts

1 cup fresh basil

1/4 teaspoon salt

1/3 cup extra-virgin olive oil

Chicken

2 tablespoons rice vinegar

1 tablespoon Dijon mustard

1 tablespoon pepper

12 chicken breasts

Sautéed spinach (optional)

To prepare the pesto, process the garlic in a food processor until finely chopped. Add the pine nuts, basil and salt and process until chopped. Add the olive oil in a fine stream, processing constantly until the mixture is incorporated. Spoon the pesto into a small bowl and cover with plastic wrap. Chill until ready to use.

To prepare the chicken, combine the pesto, vinegar, mustard and pepper in a bowl and mix well. Pour into a large sealable plastic bag. Add the chicken and seal the bag. Turn the bag several times to coat the chicken. Marinate in the refrigerator for 30 to 60 minutes. Drain the chicken, discarding the marinade. Place the chicken on a grill rack. Grill for 10 minutes or until the chicken is cooked through, turning once. Serve on a bed of sautéed spinach.

A Thyme to Entertain

Succulent Squash Bake

Moderate — Serves 8 to 10

Combine the squash and onion in a saucepan and add enough water to cover. Season lightly with salt to taste. Cook over medium heat for 5 to 7 minutes or until the squash is tender-crisp; drain thoroughly. Spoon into a bowl. Add the cheese, tomatoes with green chiles, tomato, 1/2 cup butter, the garlic powder, 1/4 teaspoon salt and the pepper and toss gently to mix. Spoon into a lightly buttered 2-quart baking dish.

Melt 1/4 cup butter in a small saucepan. Pour over the squash mixture. Sprinkle evenly with the cracker crumbs. Bake, covered with foil, at 350 degrees for 30 minutes or until bubbly and heated through. Remove the foil and bake until the top is brown. (Note: This recipe is terrific served with fish or steak and freezes well.)

2 pounds yellow squash, cut into
      1/2-inch slices
1/4 cup chopped Vidalia onion or
      other sweet onion
Salt to taste
2 cups (8 ounces) shredded
      Cheddar cheese
1 (10-ounce) can tomatoes with
      green chiles, drained
1 small tomato, chopped
      and drained
1/2 cup (1 stick) butter
Pinch of garlic powder
1/4 teaspoon salt
Dash of pepper
1/4 cup (1/2 stick) butter
1 1/2 cups cracker crumbs

Blueberry Carrot Cake with Pineapple Rum Glaze

Moderate — Serves 12

Cake

1 tablespoon butter

1 tablespoon unbleached
    all-purpose flour

2 cups unbleached all-purpose flour

2 teaspoons baking powder

2 teaspoons cinnamon

1 teaspoon baking soda

1 teaspoon salt

1 cup granulated sugar

1/2 cup packed light brown sugar

1 cup corn oil

1/4 cup walnut oil or favorite nut oil

4 eggs

4 carrots, peeled and coarsely grated

1 cup coarsely chopped walnuts

2 cups fresh blueberries, rinsed
    and drained

Pineapple Rum Glaze

1/3 cup pineapple juice

1/4 cup (1/2 stick) unsalted butter

1/4 cup granulated sugar

1/4 cup packed light brown sugar

1/4 cup dark rum

To prepare the cake, coat a nonstick 12-cup bundt pan or tube pan with the butter and sprinkle with 1 tablespoon flour. Turn the pan several times to coat with the flour and tap out any excess. Mix 2 cups flour, the baking powder, cinnamon, baking soda and salt together. Combine the granulated sugar and brown sugar in a large bowl. Whisk in the corn oil and walnut oil. Add the eggs one at a time, whisking until smooth after each addition. Stir in the carrots and walnuts. Fold in the flour mixture; do not overmix. (The batter will be thick.) Sprinkle the blueberries over the top and fold in. Spoon the batter into the prepared pan. Bake at 350 degrees for 1 hour or until the cake begins to pull away from the side of the pan and a wooden pick inserted in the center comes out clean. Cool the cake in the pan on a wire rack for 15 minutes. Invert onto a serving plate to cool completely. (Note: You may use nonstick baking spray to coat the bundt pan. Unsweetened frozen blueberries may be substituted for the fresh.)

To prepare the glaze, combine the pineapple juice, butter, granulated sugar, brown sugar and rum in a small heavy saucepan. Bring to a boil, stirring constantly. Reduce the heat and simmer for 7 minutes or until the mixture is bubbly and caramel in color. Remove from the heat and cool to room temperature. Pour over the cooled cake.

Sandy Point Sand Tarts

Moderate — Makes 2 to 3 dozen

Cream the butter in a mixing bowl. Add 1/4 cup confectioners' sugar and beat until light and fluffy. Add the flour and vanilla and mix well. Stir in the pecans. Shape into balls and press down on an ungreased cookie sheet. Bake at 225 degrees for 15 minutes. Increase the oven temperature to 275 degrees and bake for 5 minutes longer or until light brown around the edges. Do not overbake. Place additional confectioners' sugar in a shallow bowl. Carefully lift the warm cookies with a spatula and place in the confectioners' sugar. Turn the cookies in the confectioners' sugar until coated. Place on a serving plate and let stand until cooled completely. (Note: These cookies look festive stored in glass jars for the holidays and have a long shelf life.)

1 cup (2 sticks) unsalted
    butter, softened
1/4 cup confectioners' sugar
2 1/2 cups all-purpose flour, sifted
2 teaspoons vanilla extract
1 cup pecans, chopped
Confectioners' sugar for coating

The Junior League of Annapolis, Inc. is an organization of women committed to promoting voluntarism, developing the potential of women, and improving the community through the effective action and leadership of trained volunteers. Its purpose is exclusively educational and charitable. The Junior League of Annapolis and 293 leagues from the United States, Mexico, Canada, and the United Kingdom comprise the Association of Junior Leagues International. The Association of Junior Leagues International (AJLI) celebrated more than one hundred years of commitment to voluntarism in 2006. The Junior League of Annapolis celebrated more than twenty-five years of contributions to volunteer efforts in Anne Arundel County in 2006.

Sponsored by

The Junior League of Annapolis, Inc.
Board of Directors 2006–2007

CELEBRATION

GRADUATION

Graduations are timeless celebrations dating back to the twelfth century. Commencement is a time of beginnings and endings. Finally all of the hard work and studying has paid off. During the graduation ceremony you are given your diploma, and the next chapter of your life begins as you walk across the stage. Hats off to you, let the feasting begin.

Graduation Celebration

Asian Meatballs

Crab Cakes in Artichoke Saucers

Pesto and Tortellini Salad

Party Pea Pods

Sophisticated Salmon with Wild Mushroom Risotto

Almond Joy Cake

...hats off to you, let the feasting begin

Asian Meatballs

Easy — Serves 15 to 20

1/2 cup finely chopped water chestnuts

1/3 cup sliced green onions

2 garlic cloves, crushed

1 teaspoon ginger

1 (8-ounce) jar plum sauce or
hoisin sauce

1/2 to 1 (8-ounce) jar garlic
chili sauce

2 tablespoons light soy sauce

1 (38-ounce) package frozen
precooked meatballs

Combine the water chestnuts, green onions, garlic and ginger in a bowl and mix well. Mix the plum sauce, garlic chili sauce and soy sauce in a bowl. Layer the meatballs, water chestnut mixture and sauce mixture alternately in a slow cooker until all of the ingredients are used. Cook on High for 2 hours, stirring occasionally so the meatballs will heat through evenly. Reduce the heat to Low to keep warm during serving. Keep a slotted serving spoon and spoon rest nearby for serving.

Annapolis honors its graduates with a weeklong celebration of events. The U.S. Naval Academy has Commissioning Week, which includes many parties, dances, and receptions. Annapolis is filled to the brim with friends and families. The highlight of the graduation ceremony for Naval Academy graduates and guests is the flyover salute from the Blue Angels, the Navy's precision flying team.

Sponsored by **Marriott**
ANNAPOLIS WATERFRONT

Crab Cakes in Artichoke Saucers

Moderate — Serves 6 to 8

Sauté the green onions, thyme, bay leaves and cayenne pepper in the butter in a skillet for 3 minutes. Add the wine and crab meat and mix well. Remove from the heat. Discard the bay leaves. Fold in the egg and bread crumbs. Season with salt.

Place the artichoke bottoms on a baking sheet, trimming if needed to lay flat. Shape the crab meat mixture into six to eight balls and place each on an artichoke bottom. Sprinkle evenly with the Swiss cheese. Bake at 350 degrees for 10 minutes. Remove to a serving plate and top with hollandaise sauce. Garnish each with a small pinch of parsley.

1/2 bunch green onions, thinly sliced

Small pinch of fresh thyme leaves

2 bay leaves

Pinch of cayenne pepper

1/2 cup (1 stick) butter, melted

1/4 cup white wine

1 pound lump crab meat,
    drained and flaked

1 egg, beaten

1/2 cup bread crumbs

Salt to taste

6 to 8 canned artichoke bottoms

1 cup (4 ounces) shredded
    Swiss cheese

Hollandaise sauce

Chopped parsley

Pesto and Tortellini Salad

Easy — Serves 6 to 8

2 (20-ounce) packages
    cheese tortellini

1 (8-ounce) jar pesto sauce

1/2 cup white wine tarragon vinegar

1 pound asparagus, coarsely
    chopped and blanched

2 cups julienned red and yellow
    bell peppers

1/2 cup chopped pecans

1/2 cup pine nuts

Cook the tortellini using the package directions. Do not overcook. Rinse the tortellini with cold water and drain. Place the pasta in a large bowl. Whisk the pesto sauce and vinegar in a bowl until blended. Add the asparagus, bell peppers, pecans and pine nuts and mix well. Pour over the pasta and toss to coat. Chill, covered, in the refrigerator.

The Junior League of Annapolis has supported more than one hundred worthwhile projects of fellow nonprofit organizations in Anne Arundel County by awarding Community Assistance Donation Awards. The League has made donations to a bereavement center, child advocacy efforts, a drug rehabilitation program, a homeless shelter, various after-school programs, the local symphony, a domestic violence counseling program, literacy projects, intercultural arts programs, and a children's museum to name a few.

A Thyme to Entertain

Party Pea Pods

Moderate — Serves 50

Place the peas in a large heatproof bowl. Pour enough boiling water over the peas to cover. Let stand for 2 minutes to blanch. Drain the peas and place immediately in a bowl filled with ice water. Let stand for 5 minutes to stop the cooking process. Drain the peas and pat dry. Chill for 30 minutes or longer.

Combine the cream cheese, butter, half-and-half, dry mustard, garlic powder, salt and pepper in a mixing bowl and beat until smooth. Spoon the cream cheese mixture into a large plastic bag and cut off the corner at a small angle for piping or spoon into a pastry bag fitted with a decorative 1/8-inch tip.

To assemble, cut 1/4 inch from the stem end of each snow pea and gently open lengthwise. Pipe the cream cheese mixture into the pea pods and arrange on a serving plate. Chill, covered, for 4 to 24 hours. Serve cold. (Note: The cream cheese mixture may also be piped into other vegetables or onto bagel chips.)

100 fresh snow peas or sugar peas

8 ounces cream cheese, softened

1/4 cup (1/2 stick) butter, softened

2 tablespoons half-and-half

1 teaspoon dry mustard

1/4 to 1/2 teaspoon garlic powder, or to taste

1/2 teaspoon salt

1/4 teaspoon pepper, or to taste

Sophisticated Salmon with Wild Mushroom Risotto

Gourmet — Serves 6

Salmon

1¹/₂ pounds fillet of salmon, skinned
and cut into 4-ounce fillets

Salt and cracked pepper to taste

1 (17-ounce) package puff pastry

1 egg

1 tablespoon water or milk

Mushroom Ragout

1¹/₂ pounds wild mushrooms
(shiitake, morel, etc.)

1 to 2 tablespoons extra-virgin
olive oil

Splash of cognac

2 tablespoons olive oil

1 tablespoon butter

2 tablespoons minced shallots

1 teaspoon minced garlic

1 tablespoon chopped fresh herbs
(a mixture of parsley, tarragon,
sage and thyme)

To prepare the salmon, season each fillet with salt and pepper. Unroll the puff pastry and cut into six long strips 1¹/₂ inches wide. Place one fillet in the middle of each strip of pastry, perpendicular to the pastry. Wrap the pastry around the fillet and pinch together both sides about one inch or more from the ends, allowing some of the pastry to flap over to create a bow shape. Place on a nonstick tray. Beat the egg with the water in a small bowl. Brush the pastry with the egg mixture and chill in the refrigerator. Place the salmon on a baking sheet just before serving and bake at 425 degrees for 15 minutes.

To prepare the mushroom ragout, clean and slice the mushrooms. Sauté the mushrooms in small batches in 1 to 2 tablespoons hot olive oil until all of the mushrooms are brown. Increase the heat to high and return all of the mushrooms to the skillet. Add the cognac, 2 tablespoons olive oil, the butter, shallots, garlic and herbs. Sauté for a few minutes or until the shallots are soft and the cognac evaporates. Set aside until ready to serve.

A Thyme to Entertain

To prepare the risotto, heat the vegetable stock in a 3-quart stockpot and keep warm. Sauté the shallots in 2 tablespoons butter and the olive oil in a large heavy saucepan for 1 minute. Add the garlic and rice and sauté for 1 to 2 minutes. Then, add 2 to 3 cups of the warmed stock. Simmer until all of the liquid is absorbed, stirring gently. Repeat the process with the remaining stock until the rice is al dente. Season with salt and pepper. Now, add the wine and cook until the wine is absorbed, stirring constantly. If the rice is not at the desired tenderness, add more stock a little at a time to finish. Add the cream, cheese, 1 tablespoon butter, the parsley, tarragon, sage, thyme and half the mushroom ragout. (Note: The total cooking time for the rice will be 20 to 25 minutes.)

To serve, place generous portions of the risotto on serving plates. Spoon the remaining mushrooms evenly over the risotto. Top with the salmon and serve immediately.

Photograph for this recipe appears on page 105.

Risotto

4 to 6 cups vegetable stock

4 shallots, minced

2 tablespoons butter, melted

2 tablespoons extra-virgin olive oil

4 garlic cloves, minced

2 cups arborio rice

Salt and pepper to taste

1 cup white wine

1 cup cream

1/2 cup (2 ounces) grated
    Parmigiano-Reggiano

1 tablespoon butter

1/3 cup chopped fresh parsley

1 1/2 tablespoons chopped
    fresh tarragon

1 teaspoon chopped fresh sage

2 teaspoons chopped fresh thyme

Almond Joy Cake

Moderate — Serves 12 to 15

1 (2-layer) package devil's food
    cake mix
1 (12-ounce) can evaporated milk
1^1/2 cups sugar
25 large marshmallows
1 (14-ounce) package flaked coconut
1 cup sugar
^{1}/2 cup (1 stick) butter
2 cups (12 ounces) semisweet
    chocolate chips
3 ounces almonds, toasted

Prepare the cake mix and bake using the package directions for a 9x13-inch cake pan. Combine one-half of the evaporated milk and 1^1/2 cups sugar in a saucepan. Bring to a rapid boil and remove from the heat. Add the marshmallows, stirring until melted. Stir in the coconut. Pour over the cake, spreading to cover.

Combine 1 cup sugar and the remaining evaporated milk in a saucepan. Bring to a boil and remove from the heat. Add the butter and chocolate chips and stir until melted and smooth. Stir in the almonds. Pour over the coconut layer. Chill, covered, for 2 to 24 hours before serving to enhance the flavor of the cake.

Party Pink Lemonade

Easy — Serves 6 to 8

2 cups fresh lemon juice
    (about 12 lemons)
6 cups water
1 cup superfine sugar
2 tablespoons grape juice

Combine the lemon juice, water, sugar and grape juice in a pitcher and mix well. Add enough ice to fill the pitcher and serve.

A Thyme to Entertain

Maple French Toast

Easy — Serves 3 to 4

Beat the eggs in a shallow bowl until fluffy. Whisk in the milk, 1/3 cup maple syrup, the cream, nutmeg and cinnamon. Dip the bread slices into the egg mixture. Cook the bread slices on a buttered griddle for 2 to 3 minutes on each side until golden brown. Serve with warm maple syrup. (Note: The French toast may also be served with blueberry preserves thinned with lemon juice.)

2 eggs
2/3 cup milk
1/3 cup pure maple syrup
2 tablespoons heavy cream
Dash of nutmeg
Dash of cinnamon
8 slices thick bread
Pure maple syrup, warmed

Chipotle Hummus

Easy — Serves 8 to 10

Process the chick-peas, chipotle chile, bell pepper, garlic, cilantro, lemon juice, lime juice, salt and pepper in a food processor until smooth. Spoon into a serving bowl. Serve with flatbread, pita chips and/or assorted vegetables.

2 (19-ounce) cans chick-peas, drained
1 chipotle chile, roasted and chopped
1/2 cup chopped red bell pepper
3 garlic cloves
2 tablespoons chopped cilantro
1/4 cup lemon juice
1 tablespoon lime juice
1 teaspoon salt
1/8 teaspoon pepper

Chicken Alouette

Moderate — Serves 6

1 (17-ounce) package puff
    pastry, thawed
1 (4-ounce) container Alouette Garlic
    and Herbs Spreadable Cheese
6 boneless skinless chicken breasts
Salt and pepper to taste
1 egg
1 tablespoon water

Unfold the puff pastry sheets. Roll out each sheet of the puff pastry, adding 2 inches to the length and width of each. Cut one sheet into four 6x7-inch rectangles. Cut the remaining sheet into two 6x7-inch rectangles and one 6x14-inch rectangle. Spread the cheese on the six small rectangles, leaving a 1/2-inch border around the edges. Season the chicken with salt and pepper. Place one chicken breast on each of the pastry rectangles. Moisten the edges of the rectangles with water and press together lengthwise to enclose the chicken in packets. Place the packets on a greased baking sheet. Cut the remaining 6x12-inch rectangle of puff pastry into the desired shapes and place on the packets to decorate. Beat the egg with 1 tablespoon water in a bowl. Brush over the pastry packets. Place on the lower oven rack and bake at 400 degrees for 25 minutes or until golden brown.

Annapolis's other proud school is St. John's College. This liberal arts school has been known since 1937 for its "Great Books" curriculum. Students there have no majors, no academic departments, and no textbooks, and they all follow the same program. They read the classic books of the major discipline areas in chronological order from Greek to modern times and discuss them.

Maryland-Style Fried Chicken

Easy — Serves 4

Rinse the chicken and pat dry. Season the flour with the salt, pepper and paprika in a shallow dish. Beat the eggs in a shallow dish. Place the bread crumbs in a shallow dish. Heat the peanut oil to 350 degrees in a large cast-iron skillet. Coat the chicken in the flour mixture, the egg mixture and then the bread crumbs, shaking off the excess after each step. Place the chicken gently in the hot peanut oil. Fry for 35 to 45 minutes or until a meat thermometer registers 165 degrees when inserted into the chicken, turning once. Remove to a cooling rack. Adjust the seasonings to taste. (Note: For variation, try seasoning the chicken with garlic salt, Chesapeake Bay Seasoning, Cajun seasoning, etc.)

1 whole chicken, cut into pieces

3 cups all-purpose flour

1 tablespoon salt

1 tablespoon pepper

1 tablespoon paprika

2 eggs

3 cups unseasoned bread crumbs

24 ounces peanut oil

Steak Cilantro Blue

Easy — Serves 3 to 4

Place the steak on a cutting board. Rub a mixture of the white pepper and black pepper into the steak on all sides. Place on a grill rack. Grill over hot coals for 12 to 14 minutes for rare or to the desired degree of doneness, turning once. Chop the cilantro into 1-inch pieces to measure 1 1/2 to 2 cups. Sauté the cilantro in the hot olive oil in a wok over medium-high heat until wilted significantly. Add the wine. Cook until most of the wine has evaporated. Stir in the blue cheese, removing from the heat when the blue cheese begins to melt. Spoon over the hot steak and slice the steak diagonally to serve.

2 to 3 pounds choice or prime top round steak or sirloin steak, cut 1 1/2 inches thick

1 teaspoon finely ground white pepper

2 to 3 tablespoons coarse cracked black pepper, or to taste

2 bunches fresh cilantro

2 tablespoons olive oil

1/4 cup red wine

8 ounces blue cheese, crumbled

Company Potatoes

Moderate — Serves 6 to 8

6 potatoes, scrubbed

Salt to taste

1/4 cup (1/2 stick) butter, melted

1 1/2 cups (6 ounces) shredded
  Cheddar cheese

1 cup sour cream

2 green onions, chopped

1 teaspoon salt

1/4 teaspoon pepper

2 tablespoons butter, softened

1/2 cup (2 ounces) shredded
  Cheddar cheese

Place the potatoes in a large saucepan. Cover with salted water. Bring to a boil and reduce the heat. Simmer for 30 minutes or until tender. Drain the potatoes and cool slightly. Peel the potatoes and coarsely shred into a large bowl. Combine 1/4 cup butter and 1 1/2 cups cheese in a heavy saucepan. Cook over low heat until the cheese is partially melted, stirring constantly. Add the melted cheese, sour cream, green onions, 1 teaspoon salt and the pepper to the potatoes and stir to mix well. Spoon into a greased shallow 2-quart baking dish. Dot with 2 tablespoons butter and sprinkle with 1/2 cup cheese. Cover and bake at 300 degrees for 20 minutes.

Green Rice

Easy — Serves 6 to 8

1 cup long grain rice

Salt to taste

2 eggs, well beaten

3/4 cup milk

1/4 cup (1/2 stick) butter, melted

1/4 cup (1 ounce) shredded sharp
  Cheddar cheese

1 tablespoon grated onion

1/3 cup minced fresh parsley

1 teaspoon Worcestershire sauce

2/3 cup finely chopped fresh spinach

1 1/4 teaspoons salt

Cook the rice in boiling salted water in a saucepan using the package directions. Combine the cooked rice, eggs, milk, butter, cheese, onion, parsley, Worcestershire sauce, spinach and 1 1/4 teaspoons salt in a large bowl and mix well. Spoon into a greased and floured 8x8-inch baking dish. Place the baking dish in a larger shallow baking pan. Add enough water to the larger pan to measure 1 inch. Bake at 325 degrees for 45 minutes.

A Thyme to Entertain

Mud Pie

Moderate — Serves 8

Combine the cookie crumbs, milk and 1/3 cup butter in a bowl and mix well. Press the mixture over the bottom and up the side of a 9-inch pie plate. Freeze until firm. Spread the vanilla ice cream in the frozen crust and freeze until firm. Spread the coffee ice cream over the vanilla ice cream layer and freeze until firm.

Combine the remaining ingredients in a double boiler and mix well. Cook over hot water until the mixture is thick, stirring constantly. Remove from the heat to cool. Pour over the coffee ice cream layer and freeze until 10 minutes before serving.

13/4 cups chocolate cookie crumbs

1/3 cup milk

1/3 cup butter, melted

1 pint light vanilla ice cream, softened

1 pint coffee ice cream or light latte ice cream, softened

2 ounces unsweetened chocolate

1/2 cup sugar

1 (5-ounce) can evaporated milk

1 tablespoon butter

Yum-Yum Bars

Moderate — Serves 24

Combine the cake mix, oil and eggs in a large bowl and mix well. Stir in the chocolate chips, peanut butter chips and toffee pieces. Press half the mixture in the bottom of a greased 9x13-inch baking pan. Bake at 350 degrees for 10 minutes. Combine the butter, caramels and sweetened condensed milk in a medium saucepan. Cook over medium heat until the caramels are melted and the mixture is smooth, stirring occasionally. Pour over the partially baked layer. Spoon the remaining chocolate mixture over the caramel layer. (The chocolate mixture will not cover the caramel layer completely.) Bake for 25 minutes or until the top is set. Cool completely and then cut into twenty-four bars.

1 (2-layer) package chocolate cake mix

1/3 cup vegetable oil

2 eggs

2 cups (12 ounces) semisweet chocolate chips

1 cup (6 ounces) peanut butter chips

3 (1.4-ounce) bars chocolate-covered toffee, cut into pieces

1/2 cup (1 stick) butter

32 caramels

1 (14-ounce) can sweetened condensed milk

CHESAPEAKE BAY CRAB FEAST

The Chesapeake Bay blue crab is one of the most enduring symbols of Maryland cuisine. Since the mid-1800s, Maryland blue crabs have been caught commercially in the Chesapeake Bay area and are one of the most important species harvested in the Bay. Not surprisingly, locals would argue that Maryland produces the best-tasting crab meat; nowhere else in the world can you find this delicacy cooked to such perfection. Chesapeake locals regularly throw impromptu crab feasts, which are the highlight of summer entertaining in Maryland. A Maryland crab feast should be a leisurely afternoon or evening, spent with family and friends enjoying good food and conversation. Whether served up steamed on a table covered with newspaper or combined with other ingredients to create your favorite crab dish, they're a delicious part of a Chesapeake Bay summer.

Chesapeake Bay Crab Feast

Shrimp Rockefeller

Steamed Maryland Blue Crabs

Chesapeake Bay Mussels

Party Bread • Potato Salad

Ice Cream Sandwiches

...the highlight of summer entertaining in Maryland

Shrimp Rockefeller

Moderate — Serves 8 to 10

2 (10-ounce) packages frozen
    chopped spinach
1/2 cup chopped onion
1/4 cup water
1/4 teaspoon salt
3 slices white bread, trimmed and
    cut into cubes
1/2 cup (1 stick) butter
1 1/2 teaspoons Worcestershire sauce
1 teaspoon celery salt
1/2 teaspoon garlic powder
1/4 teaspoon hot red pepper sauce
1/2 cup dry bread crumbs
1/4 cup (1 ounce) grated
    Parmesan cheese
2 tablespoons butter, melted
1 1/2 pounds fresh shrimp, cooked
    and peeled
8 to 10 scallop shells (optional)

Combine the spinach, onion, water and salt in a saucepan and cook until the spinach is thawed and separates easily. Stir in the bread, 1/2 cup butter, the Worcestershire sauce, celery salt, garlic powder and hot sauce. Simmer for 10 minutes. Combine the bread crumbs, cheese and 2 tablespoons butter in a bowl and mix well; set aside. Reserve eight to ten shrimp. Divide the remaining shrimp among eight to ten scallop shells or arrange in a greased shallow baking dish. Spoon the spinach mixture on top and sprinkle with the bread crumb mixture. Top with the reserved shrimp. Bake at 400 degrees for 15 minutes. (Note: You may use two (8-ounce) packages frozen peeled cooked shrimp instead of fresh.)

A Thyme to Entertain

Steamed Maryland Blue Crabs

Easy — Makes 3 dozen

Cook the crabs in batches in boiling water in a large stockpot for 1 minute, draining and discarding the liquid after the final batch. Pour the beer into the bottom of a large crab pot with a rack. Add more beer if needed for the liquid to come level with the bottom of the rack. Layer six crabs and 6 tablespoons of the Chesapeake Bay seasoning on the rack in the prepared pan. Repeat the layers until all of the crabs and seasoning are used. Bring the beer, uncovered, to a boil and then reduce the heat. Cover and simmer for 20 minutes. Season with additional Chesapeake Bay seasoning if desired. Serve the hot crabs on a table covered in newspaper. Crack and remove the shells. Serve the crab meat plain or with vinegar and melted butter on the side for dipping. (This is a favorite recipe from our first cookbook *Of Tide & Thyme*.)

Photograph for this recipe appears on page 121.

3 dozen Maryland blue crabs

1 cup (or more) beer or water

1 cup vinegar

2 1/4 cups (or more) Chesapeake Bay seasoning

Chesapeake Bay Mussels

Moderate — Serves 4

2 garlic cloves, crushed

1/4 cup olive oil

1 tablespoon Chesapeake
    Bay seasoning

1 fish bouillon cube

2 cups boiling water

1 (14-ounce) can plum tomatoes

1 (12-ounce) bottle of light beer

35 to 40 fresh mussels

Sea salt to taste

Sauté the garlic in the hot olive oil in the bottom of a two-part steamer over low heat for 3 minutes. Stir in the Chesapeake Bay seasoning. Dissolve the bouillon cube in the boiling water and add to the garlic mixture. Increase the heat to medium. Add the tomatoes and beer and bring to a simmer. Place the mussels in a metal colander and run cold water over them. Discard any mussels that are cracked or have opened. Trim the hair-like part of the mussel that protrudes from the shell. Scrub each mussel well under the running water with a brush or by hand. Arrange the mussels in the top portion of the steamer and sprinkle with sea salt. Stack the top portion of the steamer over the bottom and cover with the lid. Steam for 10 minutes or until the mussels begin to open. Remove any that have opened and continue to steam the remaining mussels until they do. Discard any mussels that never open. Arrange the opened mussels in bowls and pour the broth over the top. Serve with French bread.

Photograph for this recipe appears on page 121.

A Thyme to Entertain

Party Bread

Easy — Serves 8 to 10

Combine the butter, onion, seasoned salt and poppy seeds in a bowl and mix well; set aside. Place the bread in the center of a foil-lined baking sheet. Cut deep diagonal slits across the bread in both directions, creating a diamond pattern. Do not cut all the way through the loaf. Spread the slits open and fill with 4 cups cheese, the mushrooms and ham. Spoon the butter mixture evenly over the top of the loaf, getting the mixture into the slits. Place a piece of foil on top and secure to the bottom piece of foil, completely incasing the loaf. Bake at 350 degrees for 45 minutes. Sprinkle with additional shredded cheese. (Note: Use any type of cheese in this recipe.)

3/4 to 1 cup (1 1/2 to 2 sticks) butter, melted
3 tablespoons chopped onion (optional)
2 teaspoons seasoned salt
1 tablespoon poppy seeds
1 loaf Italian bread
4 cups (1 pound) shredded cheese
1 (4-ounce) can sliced mushrooms, drained
1/2 to 1 cup chopped cooked ham
Shredded cheese (optional)

Potato Salad

Easy — Serves 6 to 8

1/3 cup yogurt or sour cream

1/4 cup mayonnaise

3 tablespoons Dijon mustard

1/2 cup finely chopped red onion

1 garlic clove, minced

1/2 teaspoon dill weed

1/2 teaspoon salt

1 1/2 pounds baby red potatoes, cooked and cut into quarters

8 ounces sugar snap peas, blanched

Blend the yogurt, mayonnaise and mustard in a large bowl until smooth. Stir in the onion, garlic, dill weed and salt. Add the potatoes and peas and toss gently in the dressing until evenly coated.

Photograph for this recipe appears on page 121.

Ice Cream Sandwiches

Easy — Serves 20

1 pint lemon sorbet, raspberry sorbet or green mint chocolate chip ice cream

40 shortbread cookies

Scoop 2 teaspoons of the sorbet onto half of the cookies. Top each with one of the remaining cookies and press slightly down. Smooth the edges and arrange on baking sheets. Freeze, covered, for 1 hour or until ready to serve. (Note: Choose ice cream flavor/color to coordinate with party theme.)

Photograph for this recipe appears on page 121.

A Thyme to Entertain

Miniature Crab Quiches

Moderate — Makes 2 dozen

Cut each biscuit into thirds and press into the bottom of twenty-four greased 1¾-inch muffin cups. Spoon a small amount of crab meat on top of each biscuit. Whisk the egg, cream, brandy, salt and pepper in a bowl. Divide evenly into the muffin cups. Slice the cheese into twenty-four small triangles and place one in each muffin cup. Bake at 375 degrees for 15 to 20 minutes or until golden brown. (Note: To freeze, wrap each cooled baked quiche in foil and store in the freezer. To serve, place the frozen quiche on a baking sheet and bake at 375 degrees for 10 to 12 minutes or until heated through.)

1 (8-count) can refrigerator butter flake biscuits or refrigerator dinner rolls

1 pound backfin crab meat

1 egg, lightly beaten

½ cup table cream

1½ tablespoons brandy

½ teaspoon salt

Dash of pepper

1⅓ ounces (2 block triangles) Gruyère cheese

Hot red pepper sauce to taste

Maryland Vegetable Crab Soup

Easy — Serves 6 to 8

1 bunch celery, finely chopped

4 carrots, finely chopped

2 onions, finely chopped

Vegetable oil for sautéing

1 gallon crab stock

1 gallon beef stock

1/2 cup Chesapeake Bay seasoning

1/4 cup (or more) hot red
  pepper sauce

6 potatoes, peeled and
  finely chopped

1 pound corn

1 pound lima beans

1 pound green beans, cut into
  bite-sized pieces

1 pound crab meat

Sauté the celery, carrots and onions in vegetable oil in a stockpot until softened. Add the crab stock and beef stock. Stir in the Chesapeake Bay seasoning, hot sauce, potatoes, corn, lima beans and green beans. Bring to a boil and then reduce the heat. Simmer until all of the vegetables are cooked through. Stir in the crab meat. Season with additional hot sauce if desired. (Note: Crab stock can be made from whole crabs or using a flavoring base. Use fresh Maryland jumbo lump crab meat whenever possible.)

Choosing and preparing crab meat carefully is important to the quality of the finished dish. Crab meat is available in the following forms:

- *Lump—the most expensive and includes the largest pieces from the body adjacent to the backfin; use it where appearance is important, such as crab imperial or in a crab salad.*
- *Backfin—consists of lump and some flakes; offers more versatility; great for crab cakes and crab imperial.*
- *Special—consists of flakes of white body meat without the lump; use for soups, casseroles, or dips.*
- *Claw—the brownish meat from the claws; use for soups, crab balls, or dips.*

Summer Salad

Easy — Serves 8

Combine the vinegar, safflower oil, mustard, garlic and sugar in a jar with a tight-fitting lid and seal tightly. Shake to mix. Chill until ready to use.

Combine the lettuce, artichoke hearts and sunflower seeds in a salad bowl. Add the dressing and toss until coated. Serve immediately.

1 cup rice vinegar

1 cup safflower oil

2 tablespoons Dijon mustard

1 tablespoon crushed garlic

1 teaspoon sugar

1 (12-ounce) package bibb lettuce

1 (6-ounce) jar artichoke
    hearts, sliced

Sunflower seeds to taste

Annapolis Oyster Melts

Easy — Serves 8 to 12

Shuck and drain the oysters, leaving the oyster in one-half of its shell. Place oyster side up on a rack in a broiler pan. Top each with 1 tablespoon of the barbeque sauce, 1 tablespoon of the cheese and 1 piece of the bacon. Broil on the highest oven rack for 3 to 4 minutes or until the bacon is brown and the cheese is melted. Serve immediately. (Note: The assembly of the oyster melts can be done ahead of time on the same day of service.)

Photograph for this recipe appears on the cover.

24 fresh oysters

1 1/2 cups barbeque sauce

1 1/2 cups (6 ounces) shredded
    Cheddar cheese

6 slices bacon, cut into 2-inch pieces

Rockfish Tacos

Moderate — Serves 4

1 to 1¹/2 pounds rockfish fillets

Salt and pepper to taste

Chesapeake Bay seasoning to taste

1¹/2 tablespoons olive oil

¹/2 cup diced tomato

¹/2 cup green salsa

2 tablespoons chopped fresh cilantro

1 tablespoon fresh lime juice

8 corn or flour tortillas

1 cup chopped romaine

1 cup chopped red cabbage

¹/2 cup thinly sliced red onion

¹/2 cup (2 ounces) shredded
    Monterey Jack cheese

1 avocado, sliced

Cilantro leaves

1 lime, cut into wedges

Season the rockfish with salt, pepper and Chesapeake Bay seasoning. Place in a 9x13-inch baking dish and drizzle with the olive oil. Bake at 325 degrees for 30 minutes or until the fish begins to flake. Flake the fish apart with a fork and place in a bowl. Add the tomato, salsa, 2 tablespoons cilantro and the lime juice and toss until coated. Layer the tortillas between dampened non-recycled paper towels. Microwave on High for 1 minute. Spoon the fish mixture onto each tortilla. Top with the romaine, cabbage, onion and cheese. Garnish with the avocado and a few cilantro leaves. Serve the lime wedges on the side. (Note: For a variation, use 12 ounces peeled cooked large shrimp instead of the rockfish.)

A Thyme to Entertain

Capital City Crab Cakes

Easy — Serves 2

Blend the mayonnaise and egg white in a bowl until smooth. Stir in the crackers, salt, cayenne pepper, black pepper and celery seeds. Fold in the crab meat until well combined. Chill, covered, for 1 hour. Shape the crab mixture into patties and coat with the bread crumbs. Sauté in the melted butter in a skillet over medium-high heat until cooked through and golden brown. (Note: If serving as an appetizer, shape the mixture into small round balls instead of patties.)

1 1/2 tablespoons (heaping) mayonnaise

1 egg white

6 to 9 saltine crackers, crushed

1/4 teaspoon salt

1/4 teaspoon cayenne pepper

1/8 teaspoon black pepper

1/8 teaspoon celery seeds

1 pound lump crab meat or backfin crab meat, flaked

1/4 cup seasoned bread crumbs (optional)

1 tablespoon butter

A Chesapeake Bay Crab Feast is not a fast-food affair, nor is it a formal party. A crab feast should be a leisurely afternoon or evening spent with good company and drink. It is practically a seasonal rite for most residents and visitors to the Eastern Shore of Maryland. You'll need a table covering, several rolls of paper towels, a sharp paring knife, and some wooden mallets. Having a seasoned picker to help you start is a good idea. Don't mind the mess—a few bites of the sweet meat and you'll be hooked on this Chesapeake delicacy.

Shrimp and Feta Orzo Salad

Moderate — Serves 6

1 cup orzo, cooked, rinsed
   and drained
1 1/2 teaspoons vegetable oil or
   olive oil
1 1/4 pounds large shrimp, cooked
   and peeled
1/2 cup packed chopped fresh
   dill weed
1/4 cup olive oil
2 garlic cloves, finely chopped
1/4 cup fresh lemon juice
2 tablespoons red wine vinegar
1/2 teaspoon freshly ground pepper
4 to 6 ounces crumbled feta cheese
2 or 3 tomatoes, seeded and
   chopped
12 kalamata olives, pitted
   and chopped
4 green onions, sliced

Toss the orzo with the vegetable oil in a large serving bowl until coated. Cover and chill in the refrigerator. Cut some or all of the shrimp into halves lengthwise; set aside. Process the dill weed, olive oil, garlic, lemon juice, vinegar and pepper in a food processor until blended. Add the shrimp, cheese, tomatoes, olives, green onions and the vinaigrette to the orzo and toss until combined. Cover and chill until ready to serve. Serve chilled or at room temperature.

A Thyme to Entertain

Apple Crunch

Easy — Serves 6 to 8

Combine the apples and granulated sugar in a bowl and toss to coat. Spoon the apple mixture in a 9x13-inch baking dish. Combine the brown sugar, flour, butter, salt and vanilla in a bowl and mix well. Sprinkle evenly on top of the apples. Do not stir. Bake at 350 degrees for 1 hour or until golden brown.

7 to 9 tart apples, peeled and sliced

1/2 cup granulated sugar

1 cup packed light brown sugar

1 cup all-purpose flour

1/2 cup (1 stick) butter, melted

1/4 teaspoon salt

1/4 teaspoon vanilla extract

Severn Scream Cocktail

Easy — Serves 2 to 3

Combine the orange juice, lemon-lime soda, sherbet and rum in a blender and process until smooth. Pour into cocktail glasses and serve immediately.

6 ounces orange juice

4 ounces lemon-lime soda

1/2 cup orange sherbet

Rum to taste (optional)

a DAY ON THE BAY

As the world's largest estuary, the Chesapeake Bay is a body of water bordered by the shores of Delaware, Maryland, and Virginia. Spending a day on the Chesapeake Bay is an intimate and relaxing way to visit with friends, eat good food, and soak up some sun. Long summer days lend themselves to starting early and perhaps watching some fireworks in the evening. Don't limit yourself to the tried-and-true deli sandwich. Let your creativity be your compass as you explore the numerous creeks and rivers that comprise the Chesapeake Bay while you serve your onboard guests delicious meals!

A Day on the Bay

Schooner Slammer

Shrimp Soup

Wednesday Night Race Salad

Chicken and Seafood Jambalaya

Crab and Orzo Salad

Kent Island Dessert Cheese Ball

...an intimate and relaxing visit with friends

Schooner Slammer

Easy — Serves 2

4 ounces pineapple juice

3 ounces white rum

2 ounces passion fruit juice

2 ounces heavy cream

1 ounce amaretto

1 ounce cream of coconut

Fresh pineapple pieces

Combine the pineapple juice, white rum, passion fruit juice, heavy cream, amaretto and cream of coconut in a cocktail shaker. Fill with ice and shake until well chilled. Strain into cocktail glasses. Garnish with pineapple pieces.

Shrimp Soup

Easy — Serves 8

1 small onion, minced

1 teaspoon olive oil

2 1/2 pounds cooked shrimp, chopped

4 cups milk

2 cups cream

1/4 cup (1/2 stick) butter, cut into small pieces

3 tablespoons all-purpose flour

Dash of mace

Dash of celery seeds

Sherry to taste

Salt and pepper to taste

Sauté the onion in the hot olive oil in a skillet until tender; set aside. Combine the shrimp and milk in the top of a double boiler and mix well. Cook over medium heat for 30 minutes, stirring constantly. Stir in the cream, butter, flour, mace, celery seeds and sherry. Season with salt and pepper. Cook for 15 to 20 minutes or until heated through, stirring constantly. Add additional sherry if desired just before serving.

Wednesday Night Race Salad
Moderate — Serves 6 to 8

Place the eggs in a saucepan and cover with cold water. Bring to a boil. Cover with a lid and remove from the heat. Let the eggs stand in the hot water for 10 minutes; drain. Chill the eggs until cool. Peel and chop the eggs and set aside. Cook the bacon in a skillet over medium-high heat until cooked through and crisp; drain. Crumble the bacon and set aside. Process the sugar, vinegar, green onion, mustard, celery seeds, salt and pepper in a blender until smooth. Add the oil gradually, processing constantly at high speed until incorporated. Combine the spinach, romaine, mushrooms and croutons in a large salad bowl. Add the eggs and bacon and toss to mix. Add the dressing to taste and toss to coat. Serve immediately.

Photograph for this recipe appears on page 137.

6 eggs

8 ounces sliced bacon

2/3 cup sugar

1/3 cup cider vinegar

1 green onion, coarsely chopped

1 tablespoon Dijon mustard

1 teaspoon celery seeds

1 teaspoon salt

1/2 teaspoon pepper

1 cup vegetable oil

1 pound spinach leaves, torn

1 pound romaine, torn

1/4 cup sliced fresh mushrooms

3 ounces croutons

Whether you're rounding the marks in a regatta or simply seeing where the wind will take you, sailing and the Chesapeake Bay have long been tied to each other. In today's go-fast world you can still find sailors trimming their jib, pulling halyards, or simply recounting their tall tales at local watering holes. At the center of this obsession is Annapolis, the self-proclaimed sailing capital of the world! The news of Annapolis being named the home for the Sailing Hall of Fame provides the legitimacy the sailing community has been looking for.

Chicken and Seafood Jambalaya

Moderate — Serves 4

2 bay leaves

1 1/2 teaspoons dried oregano

1 1/2 teaspoons salt

1 1/4 teaspoon white pepper

1 teaspoon cayenne pepper

1 teaspoon black pepper

3/4 teaspoon dried thyme

2 1/2 tablespoons chicken fat,
  beef fat or pork lard

2/3 cup chopped tasso or
  smoked ham

1/2 cup chopped andouille

1 cup chopped celery

3/4 cup chopped green bell pepper

1/2 cup chopped onion

1/2 cup bite-size chicken pieces

1 1/2 teaspoons minced garlic

4 tomatoes, peeled and chopped

3/4 cup canned tomato sauce

2 cups seafood stock

1/2 cup chopped green onions

2 cups rice

1 1/2 dozen peeled medium shrimp

1 1/2 dozen oysters in liquor

Combine the bay leaves, oregano, salt, white pepper, cayenne pepper, black pepper and thyme in a bowl and mix well; set aside. Heat the chicken fat in a 4-quart saucepan over medium heat. Add the tasso and andouille and sauté for 5 to 8 minutes or until crisp. Add the celery, bell pepper and onion. Sauté for 5 minutes or until tender but firm, scraping the bottom of the saucepan well.

Add the chicken. Increase the heat to high and cook for 1 minute, stirring constantly. Reduce the heat to medium and add the seasoning mixture and garlic. Cook for 3 minutes, stirring constantly and scraping the bottom of the saucepan frequently. Stir in the tomatoes and cook for 5 to 8 minutes or until the chicken is cooked through. Add the tomato sauce and cook for 7 minutes, stirring frequently. Add the seafood stock and bring to a boil. Stir in the green onions and cook for 2 minutes, stirring once or twice. Add the rice, shrimp and oysters and stir well; remove from the heat. Spoon into an 9x13-inch baking pan and cover tightly with foil. Bake at 350 degrees for 20 to 30 minutes or until the rice is al dente. Remove the bay leaves. Serve immediately.

A Thyme to Entertain

Crab and Orzo Salad

Moderate — Serves 8 to 10

Reserve four of the artichoke hearts. Chop the remaining artichoke hearts; set aside. Drain the crab meat and flake; set aside. Cook the orzo in boiling salted water until al dente. Drain the orzo and rinse under cold water. Spoon into a serving bowl and set aside. Combine the reserved artichoke hearts, vinegar, shallot, garlic, basil, mustard and oregano in a blender and process until smooth. Add the oil in a fine stream, processing constantly at high speed until incorporated. Stir 1 cup of the vinaigrette into the orzo. Add the chopped artichokes, sun-dried tomatoes, green onions, crab meat and parsley and toss gently to combine. Season with salt and pepper to taste. Serve with the remaining vinaigrette on the side.

1 (6-ounce) jar quartered marinated artichoke hearts, drained
1 pound jumbo lump crab meat
1 pound orzo
1/2 cup white wine vinegar
1 shallot, chopped
2 garlic cloves
2 basil leaves
1 teaspoon Dijon mustard
1 teaspoon dried oregano
3/4 cup olive oil
10 drained oil-pack sun-dried tomatoes, sliced
1 bunch green onions, sliced
2 tablespoons chopped parsley

Kent Island Dessert Cheese Ball

Easy — Serves 10 to 12

Combine the raisins and rum in a small saucepan. Cook over low heat for 10 to 12 minutes or until most of the rum has evaporated. Remove from the heat and pour into a bowl. Add the cream cheese, pecans, pineapple and curry powder and mix well. Shape the mixture into a large ball. Roll in the coconut, coating completely. Place on a serving plate and pour chutney over the top. Serve with thin gingersnaps. (Note: Chopped macadama nuts may be substituted for the chopped pecans.)

1/4 cup chopped raisins or dates
1/4 cup dark rum
8 ounces cream cheese, softened
1 cup chopped pecans
1/4 cup drained crushed pineapple (optional)
1 teaspoon curry powder, or to taste
1 cup shredded coconut, toasted
Mango or peach chutney

Ahoy Skipper Sipper

Moderate — Serves 4 to 6

6 cups yellow or pink lemonade

2 cups vodka

2 to 3 trays ice cubes

3 tablespoons lime juice

Pink sugar

Lemon peel twists

Process the lemonade, vodka and ice in a blender until the ice is crushed. Place the lime juice and sugar in separate shallow bowls. Dip the rims of four to six cocktail glasses into the lime juice and immediately into the sugar. Fill the cocktail glasses with the frozen drink and garnish with lemon peel twists.

Fresh Guacamole

Easy — Serves 6 to 8

2 avocados

4 teaspoons fresh lime juice

1 large plum tomato, seeded
    and chopped

1 tablespoon chopped red onion

2 tablespoons chopped fresh cilantro

Salt and pepper to taste

Dash of hot red pepper sauce, or
    minced jalapeño chile to taste

Cut the avocados lengthwise around the seed and separate into halves. Remove the seed. Scoop out the avocado with a spoon and place in a bowl. Add the lime juice and coarsely mash with a fork. Fold in the tomato, onion and cilantro. Season with salt, pepper and hot sauce. Serve at room temperature within 2 hours of preparing.

One of the best-known sailing traditions in Annapolis is the Wednesday Night Series hosted by the Annapolis Yacht Club. Every Wednesday from June to September local sailors exchange their business suits for sailing shorts as they compete for bragging rights. It's quite a sight to watch as the fleet navigates the waters of Spa Creek with spinnakers flying and a dramatic finish at the bridge.

A Thyme to Entertain

Artichoke Cakes with Creole Rémoulade

Moderate — Makes 2 dozen

To prepare the rémoulade, combine the mayonnaise, horseradish, mustard, onion, Worcestershire sauce and lemon juice in a bowl and mix well. Stir in the salt, black pepper, cayenne pepper and hot sauce. Chill, covered, until ready to serve.

To prepare the artichoke cakes, squeeze the artichokes between paper towels to remove any excess liquid. Place the artichokes in a bowl. Add the eggs, bread crumbs, bell pepper and green onions and mix well. Combine the mayonnaise, cream, lemon juice, mustard, Worcestershire sauce and salt in a bowl and blend until smooth. Add the artichoke mixture and stir gently until combined. Chill, covered, for 2 hours.

Scoop the artichoke mixture into 1 1/2-inch balls. Cook in a lightly oiled nonstick skillet for 2 to 2 1/2 minutes on each side or until golden brown and slightly set. Remove from the skillet and place on a lightly greased baking sheet. Bake at 400 degrees for 10 to 12 minutes or until cooked through and set. Serve with the Creole rémoulade.

Creole Rémoulade

2 cups mayonnaise

3 tablespoons horseradish

2 tablespoons Creole mustard

2 tablespoons grated onion

1 tablespoon white wine
    Worcestershire sauce

1 tablespoon lemon juice

1/4 teaspoon salt

1/4 teaspoon black pepper

1/4 teaspoon cayenne pepper

1/4 teaspoon hot red pepper sauce

Artichoke Cakes

3 (14-ounce) cans artichoke hearts,
    drained and chopped

2 eggs, lightly beaten

1 cup lightly packed soft
    bread crumbs

1/2 cup chopped red bell pepper

2 tablespoons chopped green onions

3/4 cup mayonnaise

1/4 cup whipping cream

2 tablespoons fresh lemon juice

2 teaspoons Dijon mustard

1 teaspoon Worcestershire sauce

1 teaspoon salt

Fabulous Marinated Shrimp

Easy — Serves 14

2 to 3 pounds medium shrimp,
    cooked, peeled and deveined

2 (14-ounce) cans hearts of
    palm, drained

2 (14-ounce) cans artichoke
    hearts, drained

1 pint cherry tomatoes (optional)

3/4 cup olive oil

1/4 cup tarragon vinegar

2 tablespoons water

1 1/2 teaspoons dry mustard

1 teaspoon sugar

2 garlic cloves, crushed

1 1/2 teaspoons salt

1/2 teaspoon pepper

Combine the shrimp, hearts of palm, artichokes and tomatoes in a container with a tight-fitting lid. Combine the olive oil, vinegar, water, dry mustard, sugar, garlic, salt and pepper in a jar with a tight-fitting lid and seal tightly. Shake to mix. Pour the marinade over the shrimp mixture and toss until coated. Cover with the lid. Marinate in the refrigerator for 8 to 10 hours, stirring or shaking the container to mix two or three times. Drain the shrimp mixture, discarding the marinade. Place in a serving bowl and use wooden picks to serve.

Another lively sailing event is the annual Hospice Cup Regatta, America's largest charity regatta. The Regatta has been run for over twenty-five years and has raised over $6.5 million, with proceeds directly benefiting participating hospices. The Chesapeake Bay race serves as a qualifying race for the National Hospice Regatta Championship. By supporting the Hospice Cup, no patient or family will need to pay any out-of-pocket expenses when seeking the services of a participating hospice. Hospices assist terminally ill patients in carrying on pain-free lives with compassion, dignity, and comfort.

A Thyme to Entertain

Weems Creek Apricot Chicken

Easy — Serves 4

Combine the preserves, salad dressing, soup mix and margarine in a bowl and mix well. Coat the chicken in flour, shaking off any excess. Place the chicken in a baking dish and pour the sauce over the top. Bake at 350 degrees for 40 minutes or until the chicken is cooked through. (Note: You may use Catalina dressing instead of Russian dressing.)

1 (10-ounce) jar apricot preserves

1 (8-ounce) bottle Russian
    salad dressing

1 envelope onion soup mix

1/2 cup (1 stick) margarine, melted

All-purpose flour for dredging

4 boneless skinless chicken breasts

White Corn Salad

Easy — Serves 8 to 10

Combine the corn, tomatoes, green chiles, cucumber and cilantro in a large bowl and toss to mix. Mix the mayonnaise, sour cream and vinegar in a small bowl until smooth. Add to the corn mixture and toss to coat well. Add the cheese and green onions and toss to combine. Season with salt and white pepper just before serving. (Note: You may use three 11-ounce cans white corn, drained, instead of the frozen corn.)

5 to 6 cups frozen white corn

2 cups halved cherry tomatoes

2 (4-ounce) cans diced green
    chiles, drained

1/2 cucumber, peeled and chopped

1 to 2 tablespoons chopped fresh
    cilantro (optional)

3 tablespoons mayonnaise

3 tablespoons sour cream

2 tablespoons rice wine vinegar

1 1/2 cups (6 ounces) shredded
    smoked Gouda cheese or
    Cheddar cheese

1 cup chopped green onion tops

1 teaspoon salt, or to taste

1/2 teaspoon white pepper

Gingered Sweet Potatoes

Easy — Serves 4 to 6

2 pounds sweet potatoes, peeled

1/2 cup dark rum

1/2 cup crushed fresh pineapple

1/3 cup water

1/4 cup sugar

1/4 cup raisins

3 tablespoons butter

1 tablespoon grated fresh ginger

1/4 teaspoon cinnamon

1/4 teaspoon ground allspice

Boil the sweet potatoes in water to cover in a stockpot until cooked through; drain. Slice the sweet potatoes and place in a serving bowl. Combine the rum, pineapple, water, sugar, raisins and butter in a saucepan. Stir in the ginger, cinnamon and allspice. Bring to a boil and reduce the heat. Simmer until the sauce is thickened, stirring frequently. Pour over the sweet potatoes and serve immediately.

Rocky Road Squares

Easy — Makes 40 squares

1 (14-ounce) can sweetened
  condensed milk

2 cups (12 ounces) semisweet
  chocolate chips

2 tablespoons butter

2 cups dry-roasted peanuts

1 (10-ounce) package
  miniature marshmallows

Combine the sweetened condensed milk, chocolate chips and butter in a microwave-safe dish. Microwave on High at 30-second intervals until melted and smooth, stirring after each interval. Combine the peanuts and marshmallows in a large bowl. Fold in the chocolate mixture. Spread into a waxed paper-lined 9x13-inch baking pan. Chill for 2 hours or until firm. Invert the pan onto a flat service and lift the pan away. Peel off the waxed paper and cut the candy into squares. Cover and store at room temperature.

Junior League of Annapolis Cookies

Easy — Makes about 2 dozen

Combine the oats, flour, baking soda and salt in a bowl and mix well. Cream the butter and brown sugar in a mixing bowl until light and fluffy. Add the eggs one at a time, beating constantly. Add the dry ingredients gradually, beating constantly. Stir in the cranberries and white chocolate. Drop by teaspoonfuls onto an ungreased cookie sheet. Bake at 375 degrees for 10 to 12 minutes or until golden brown. Cool slightly on the cookie sheet. Remove to a wire rack to cool completely.

2 cups quick-cooking oats

2 cups all-purpose flour

1 teaspoon baking soda

1/2 teaspoon salt

1 cup (2 sticks) butter, softened

1 cup packed brown sugar

2 extra-large eggs

1 1/2 cups sweetened
    dried cranberries

1 cup (6 ounces) white chocolate
    chunks or chips

The Junior League of Annapolis, Inc. (JLA) has been instrumental in public policy and legislation through its Public Advocacy Committee. JLA members have advocated for domestic violence awareness, children's rights, smoking cessation on school property, curtailing children's ability to purchase tobacco products, requiring use of seat belts, child safety seats, bicycle helmets, and safe havens for abandoned newborns. In 2000, for example, the League supported issues dealing with domestic violence, specifically Ex Parte Orders, Surrender of Firearms, Responsible Gun Safety, Inauguration of the Child Safety and Substance Abuse Treatment Services, and the Working Parents Opportunity Acts. In 2003 the League executed radio and television public service campaigns for a little-known law, Safe Haven (for the safe abandonment of newborns).

TAILGATES TO TOUCHDOWNS

Tailgating, a widely anticipated weekend engagement in communities across Maryland, allows fans to enjoy food, sport, and socializing simultaneously. From Navy Marine-Corps Memorial Stadium in Annapolis to Byrd Stadium in College Park, supporters gather throughout the autumn and spring seasons to cheer their teams to victory. Your party is sure to score with all of your friends if you prepare a delicious spread of cuisine that offers a variety of flavor and libations. And whether you are supporting the Blue and Gold or the Maryland Terps, be sure to keep your team colors in mind when decorating for the festivities!

TAILGATES
TO
TOUCHDOWNS

REDSKINS PUNCH

RAVENS PARTY RYES

VEGETARIAN CHILI CON QUESO

SHISH KABOBS

NAVY BAKED BEANS

TERRAPINS CARAMEL BROWNIES

...enjoy food, sport, and socializing simultaneously

Redskins Punch

Easy — Serves 6 to 8

1 (32-ounce) bottle red fruit punch

1¹/2 cups light rum

1¹/2 cups dark rum

1 (6-ounce) can frozen limeade
   concentrate, thawed

1 (6-ounce) can frozen orange juice
   concentrate, thawed

Combine the fruit punch, light rum, dark rum, limeade concentrate and orange juice concentrate in a large pitcher and stir well. Serve in glasses over ice.

Ravens Party Ryes

Easy — Serves 15

1 pound hot bulk pork sausage

1 pound ground beef

1 pound Velveeta cheese,
   cut into cubes

2 loaves party rye bread

Brown the sausage and ground beef in a skillet, stirring until crumbly; drain. Return the ground beef mixture to the skillet and stir in the cheese. Cook until the cheese is melted, stirring constantly. Spread the ground beef mixture on the slices of bread and arrange on baking sheets. Place the baking sheets in the freezer and freeze until firm. Place in a sealable plastic bag and return to the freezer until ready to use. To serve, place the frozen party ryes on a baking sheet and bake at 400 degrees for 10 minutes.

A Thyme to Entertain

Vegetarian Chile con Queso

Easy — Serves 6 to 8

Sauté the onion, red pepper, chipotle chiles and garlic in the hot olive oil in a large saucepan for 5 minutes. Stir in the chili powder and cumin and cook for 1 minute. Add the beans and mix well. Add enough of the stock to cover. Season with pepper. Bring to a boil and boil for 10 minutes. Reduce the heat and simmer, covered, for 50 minutes or until the beans are tender, adding more stock as needed to cover. Stir in the cheese one handful at a time. Season with salt. Serve as a dip with tortilla chips or as an entrée over rice.

(Note: Use a combination of kidney beans, black beans and pinto beans to add color to the dish. You may use two drained and rinsed 15-ounce cans of beans instead of the dry. For a variation, add chopped summer squash halfway through the simmering process or add whole grains, such as brown rice or oat groats, when the beans are added.)

1 onion, chopped

1 fire-roasted red pepper, chopped

1 or 2 chipotle chiles, chopped

2 or 3 garlic cloves, crushed

3 tablespoons olive oil

1 tablespoon chili powder

1 teaspoon cumin

2 cups dried red kidney beans,
    black beans or pinto beans,
    soaked and drained

4 cups (or more) vegetable
    stock or water

Freshly ground pepper to taste

1 pound sharp Cheddar
    cheese, shredded

Salt to taste

Hot cooked rice (optional)

Looking for something different? The Maryland Renaissance Festival is a re-creation of a sixteenth-century English village, honoring Henry VIII. Feast on a giant turkey leg and a pint of ale, watch an authentic jousting tournament, purchase period crafts, and enjoy the entertainment of wandering performers. There is something for everyone.

Shish Kabobs

Easy — Serves 4

1/3 cup packed brown sugar

1 cup Worcestershire sauce

1 cup soy sauce

1 tablespoon minced garlic

1 (46-ounce) can pineapple juice

4 boneless skinless chicken breasts

1 large zucchini

1 large yellow squash

1 onion

1 large green bell pepper

1 large red bell pepper

15 cherry tomatoes

Mushrooms, cut into halves

Combine the brown sugar, Worcestershire sauce, soy sauce, garlic and pineapple juice in a large bowl and whisk until combined. Cut the chicken into bite-size pieces and add to the marinade. Cut the zucchini, squash, onion and bell peppers into large pieces and add to the marinade. Add the tomatoes and mushrooms to the marinade. Toss until the chicken and all of the vegetables are coated well with the marinade. Marinate, covered, in the refrigerator for 2 to 3 hours. Drain the chicken and vegetables, discarding the marinade. Thread the chicken and vegetables alternately onto skewers. Place on a grill rack and grill for 15 to 30 minutes or until the chicken is cooked through and the vegetables are tender. (Note: For a variation, use shrimp or steak instead of the chicken.)

Photograph for this recipe appears on page 151.

A Thyme to Entertain

Navy Baked Beans

Easy — Serves 8 to 10

Combine the baked beans, navy beans, liqueur, brown sugar, chili sauce, mustard and molasses in a bowl and mix well. Pour the mixture into a large baking dish and chill, covered, for 4 to 12 hours. Bake at 375 degrees for 1 hour.

3 (16-ounce) cans baked beans

1 (10-ounce) can navy beans

1 cup Kahlúa

1/4 cup packed brown sugar

1/4 cup chili sauce

1 tablespoon mustard

1 tablespoon molasses

Terrapins Caramel Brownies

Easy — Serves 24 to 32

Combine the cake mix, butter and 1/3 cup evaporated milk in a bowl and mix well. Spread half the batter into a lightly greased 9x13-inch baking pan. Bake at 350 degrees for 8 to 10 minutes or until slightly set. Combine the caramels and 1/2 cup evaporated milk in a saucepan. Cook over medium heat until the caramels are melted, stirring frequently. Remove the baking pan from the oven and immediately sprinkle evenly with the chocolate chips. Pour the caramel mixture evenly over the chocolate chips. Spread the remaining batter over the top to cover the chocolate and caramel, pressing by hand to flatten. (The top will have holes like a streusel.) Bake for 16 to 20 minutes or until the brownies test done. Cool completely on a wire rack. Chill until ready to serve.

1 (2-layer) package German
   chocolate cake mix

3/4 cup (1 1/2 sticks) butter, melted

1/3 cup evaporated milk

1 (12-ounce) bag caramels

1/2 cup evaporated milk

2 cups (12 ounces) chocolate chips

Strawberry-Peach Daiquiris

Easy — Serves 4

2 cups fresh strawberries

1/4 cup sugar

3 ounces rum

1 ounce peach schnapps

1 teaspoon lemon juice

1/2 cup ice

Combine the strawberries, sugar, rum, peach schnapps and lemon juice in a blender. Top with the ice and process until smooth. Pour the daiquiri mixture into sugar-rimmed margarita glasses.

Buffalo Wing Dip

Easy — Serves 10 to 12

4 or 5 boneless skinless chicken breasts

1 (12-ounce) jar hot red pepper sauce

16 ounces cream cheese, softened

1 1/2 (12-ounce) jars blue cheese
    salad dressing

8 ounces mozzarella cheese, shredded

Boil the chicken in water to cover in a large heavy saucepan for 20 to 30 minutes or until cooked through. Shred the chicken with a fork into bite-size pieces and place in a bowl. Pour the hot sauce over the chicken and marinate, covered, in the refrigerator for 8 to 10 hours. Layer the cream cheese, undrained chicken, salad dressing and mozzarella cheese in a 9x13-inch baking dish. Bake at 350 degrees for 30 minutes. Serve with celery sticks or tortilla chips.

A Thyme to Entertain

Game Day Cheese Sandwiches

Easy — Serves 15 to 20

Combine the cheese spread, margarine, Worcestershire sauce, dill weed, Beau Monde seasoning and hot sauce in a bowl and mix well. Spread the cheese mixture between the layers of a stack of three bread slices and over the top and sides. Repeat with the remaining bread and cheese mixture. Cut each stack into quarters. Place the stacks on a baking sheet and freeze until the cheese is hardened. Bake at 350 degrees 15 to 20 minutes or until golden brown.

2 (5-ounce) jars Old English
    cheese spread
1 cup (2 sticks) margarine, softened
3/4 teaspoon Worcestershire sauce
3/4 teaspoon dill weed
1/2 teaspoon Beau Monde seasoning
1/2 teaspoon hot red pepper sauce
1 loaf thinly sliced bread,
    crusts removed

Tomato Crab Salsa

Easy — Serves 8 to 10

Cut the tomatoes into halves lengthwise and remove the seeds. Chop into 1/4-inch pieces and place in a bowl. Add the crab meat, scallions, cilantro, olive oil, oregano, garlic, lime juice and jalapeño chile and toss until combined. Serve at room temperature within 4 hours of preparing.

4 large plum tomatoes
8 ounces fresh crab meat
1/2 cup chopped scallions
1/4 cup chopped cilantro
1 tablespoon olive oil
1 tablespoon chopped fresh oregano
2 garlic cloves, minced
2 teaspoons fresh lime juice
1 teaspoon minced jalapeño chile
Salt and pepper to taste

Spicy Chicken Chile Soup

Easy — Serves 4

1 bunch green onions, chopped

2 teaspoons olive oil

2 cups shredded cooked chicken

1 (15-ounce) can kidney
　beans, drained

1 (14-ounce) can Mexican
　stewed tomatoes

1 (14-ounce) can chicken broth

1 (8-ounce) can whole kernel
　corn, drained

1 (4-ounce) can chopped green chiles

2 teaspoons chili powder

1/2 cup plus 2 tablespoons chopped
　fresh cilantro

Sauté the green onions in the hot olive oil in a large heavy saucepan for 2 minutes. Stir in the chicken, kidney beans, tomatoes, broth, corn, green chiles and chili powder. Bring to a boil and then reduce the heat. Simmer, covered, for 10 minutes. Stir in 1/2 cup of the cilantro. Simmer for 5 minutes. To serve, ladle into soup bowls and garnish with the remaining 2 tablespoons cilantro. (Note: You may use a purchased rotisserie chicken for the cooked chicken. To use, shred the chicken, discarding the skin and bones.)

Located at the famous City Dock, you'll see the Kunta Kinte-Alex Haley Memorial, which honors the site where the young African made famous in Alex Haley's "Roots," was sold into slavery in the eighteenth century. This life-size sculpture of Alex Haley reading to children is the only memorial in the United States that commemorates the actual name and place of arrival of an enslaved African. It is in an area currently visited by nearly one million people each year.

A Thyme to Entertain

Chicken and Black Bean Soup

Moderate — Serves 4

Sauté the carrots, celery, onion and broccoli stems in 1/4 cup melted butter in a heavy saucepan for 5 minutes. Stir in the thyme, oregano and basil and cook for 5 minutes. Add the wine and stir to deglaze the pan. Add the broth and cook until the liquid is reduced by one-third. Add the chicken, black beans, broccoli florets, Worcestershire sauce and Tabasco sauce and simmer for 5 minutes. Add the cream and simmer for 5 minutes. Season with salt and pepper. Add 1/4 cup butter one piece at a time, stirring well after each addition until melted. Serve immediately. (Note: If a thicker consistency is desired, you may stir in a mixture of 2 tablespoons cornstarch and a small amount of water prior to adding the butter.)

1/2 cup chopped carrots

1/2 cup chopped celery

1/2 cup chopped onion

1 cup chopped peeled
     broccoli stems

1/4 cup (1/2 stick) unsalted
     butter, melted

2 teaspoons dried thyme

2 teaspoons dried oregano

1 teaspoon dried sweet basil

1/4 cup dry white wine

4 cups chicken broth, heated

1 cup chopped cooked chicken

1 cup rinsed drained canned
     black beans

1 cup broccoli florets

1 tablespoon Worcestershire sauce

1/2 teaspoon Tabasco sauce

2 cups heavy cream

Salt and pepper to taste

1/4 cup (1/2 stick) unsalted butter,
     cut into small pieces

Fillets of Beef with Stilton-Portobello Sauce

Easy — Serves 6

6 (6-ounce) beef tenderloin fillets

2 teaspoons chopped fresh tarragon

1/2 teaspoon freshly ground pepper

5 tablespoons butter or margarine

8 ounces portobello caps, sliced

1/3 cup dry red wine

1/2 cup sour cream

3 ounces Stilton cheese, crumbled, or
    good-quality creamy blue cheese

Sprigs of fresh tarragon

Season the beef with 2 teaspoons tarragon and the pepper. Cook in 2 tablespoons of the butter in a skillet for 4 to 5 minutes on each side or to the desired degree of doneness. Remove from the skillet. Add the remaining butter and mushrooms to the skillet. Sauté until tender. Add the wine. Simmer for 1 to 2 minutes, stirring to deglaze the pan. Stir in the sour cream and 1/4 cup of the cheese. Cook until melted, stirring constantly. Arrange the beef on a serving platter. Drizzle with the sauce and sprinkle with the remaining cheese. Garnish with tarragon.

Vodka Pasta with Clams

Moderate — Serves 4

1 1/2 pounds littleneck clams

Bread crumbs

1 cup chopped onion

1/4 teaspoon red pepper

2 tablespoons olive oil

1/2 cup vodka

3/4 cup whipping cream

3/4 cup tomato sauce

2 teaspoons dried basil

8 ounces proscuitto, chopped

8 ounces penne, cooked

1/3 cup grated asiago cheese

2 tablespoons fresh parsley

Place the clams in water to cover in a bowl. Sprinkle with a small amount of bread crumbs. (The bread crumbs will cause the clams to open their shells a little which helps to get the grit, dirt or sand out.) Soak for 15 minutes; drain. Rinse the clams and clean well. Sauté the onion and red pepper in the hot olive oil in a heavy saucepan over medium heat until tender. Reduce the heat and add the vodka. Flambé until the flame subsides. Increase the heat and add the cream. Boil until the sauce thickens, stirring constantly. Stir in the tomato sauce, basil and proscuitto. Add the clams and cook until the clams open; discard any unopened clams. Add the pasta and cheese and toss gently to combine. Garnish with the parsley. Serve immediately.

A Thyme to Entertain

Blue Cheese Potatoes

Easy — Serves 4 to 6

Place the potatoes in a large heavy saucepan and cover with cold water. Bring to a boil and boil for 15 minutes or until tender. Drain the potatoes and place in a bowl. Add the butter and green onions and toss until coated. Whisk the cream and flour in a saucepan until combined. Stir in the cheese. Cook over medium heat until thickened, stirring constantly. Stir in the salt and pepper. Pour over the potato mixture and toss until coated. Sprinkle with the bacon, parsley and chives. Serve immediately.

2 pounds new potatoes,
    cut into quarters
1 tablespoon butter or margarine
3/4 cup chopped green onions
3/4 cup whipping cream
1 tablespoon all-purpose flour
2 ounces blue cheese, crumbled
1/4 teaspoon salt
1/4 teaspoon pepper
6 slices bacon, crisp-cooked
    and crumbled
1 tablespoon chopped fresh parsley
1 tablespoon minced chives

Orange Almond Crisps

Easy — Makes 4 dozen

Cream the confectioners' sugar, butter and orange zest in a mixing bowl until light and fluffy. Cut the ladyfingers into halves horizontally. Spread the cut sides with the orange mixture and place cut side up on an ungreased baking sheet. Sprinkle with the almonds. Bake at 275 degrees for 15 to 20 minutes or until golden brown. Cool and store in an airtight container.

1 cup confectioners' sugar
1/2 cup (1 stick) butter, softened
Grated zest of 2 oranges
2 (3-ounce) packages ladyfingers
1/2 cup sliced almonds

AUTUMN's
bounty

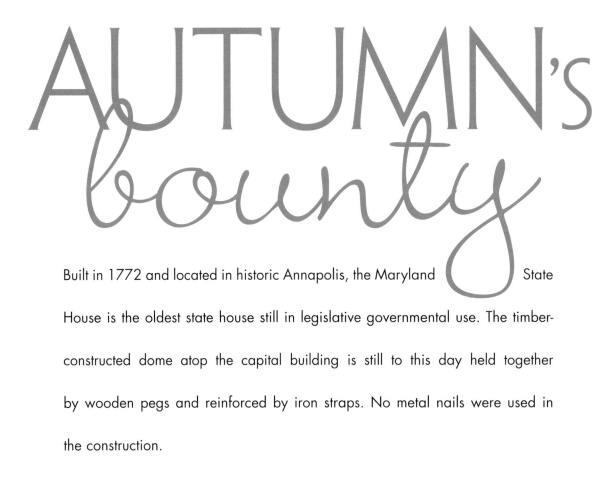

Built in 1772 and located in historic Annapolis, the Maryland State House is the oldest state house still in legislative governmental use. The timber-constructed dome atop the capital building is still to this day held together by wooden pegs and reinforced by iron straps. No metal nails were used in the construction.

Situated in the center of State Circle, the State House is a major tourist attraction. In the fall you will find school groups touring the site, Annapolitans leisurely lunching atop a picnic blanket on the manicured lawn, and students studying the detailed architecture. Don't miss the annual State House by Candlelight Tour in early December.

Autumn's Bounty

City Dock Chocolate Martini

Chicken Curry Dip

Smoky Autumn Salad

Pumpkin Soup

Racks of Lamb with Mustard Coating

Green Beans with Roquefort and Walnuts

Pumpkin Flan

...leisurely lunching atop a picnic blanket

City Dock Chocolate Martini

Easy — Serves 1

1 ounce half-and-half or heavy cream

1 ounce dark chocolate liqueur

1/2 ounce crème de cacao

1/2 ounce vodka

Fresh strawberries

Combine the half-and-half, dark chocolate liqueur, crème de cacao and vodka in a cocktail shaker. Top off with ice and shake until well chilled. Strain into a martini glass. Garnish with strawberries.

Chicken Curry Dip

Easy — Serves 10 to 12

8 ounces cream cheese, softened

1 cup cottage cheese

1/4 cup sour cream

2 teaspoons curry powder

1/3 cup chopped green onions

1/2 cup Major Grey's chutney

1/3 cup chopped raisins (optional)

1/3 cup shredded coconut

1 cup chopped cooked chicken

1/2 cup chopped salted dry-roasted
    peanuts

Combine the cream cheese, cottage cheese, sour cream and curry powder in a food processor and process until smooth. Spread in the bottom of a pie plate. Reserve a small amount of the green onions for garnishing. Layer the chutney, remaining green onions, raisins, coconut, chicken and peanuts in the order listed over the cream cheese mixture. Sprinkle the reserved green onions on top. Chill, covered, for 3 to 10 hours. Serve with crackers.

Smoky Autumn Salad

Easy — Serves 6

Combine the vinegar, maple syrup, olive oil and pepper in a large salad bowl and whisk until combined. Add the spinach, apples, cheese and pecans and toss until coated. Serve immediately.

1/4 cup balsamic vinegar

1/4 cup maple syrup

1/4 cup olive oil

1/4 teaspoon freshly ground pepper

12 ounces baby spinach leaves

2 large Granny Smith apples, cored and thinly sliced

1 cup (4 ounces) shredded smoked mozzarella cheese or smoked Gouda cheese

1/2 cup chopped pecans, toasted

Pumpkin Soup

Easy — Serves 4

Sauté the shallots in the butter in a heavy saucepan over medium heat for 5 minutes. Stir in the pumpkin and brown sugar. Stir in the broth and bring to a boil. Reduce the heat and simmer for 20 minutes. Stir in the cream and nutmeg. Season with salt and pepper. Ladle into soup bowls and garnish with almonds.

2 shallots, minced

2 tablespoons butter, melted

1 (26-ounce) can pumpkin purée

1 tablespoon brown sugar

4 cups chicken broth

1/2 cup heavy cream

Pinch of nutmeg

Salt and pepper to taste

Chopped almonds

Racks of Lamb with Mustard Coating

Moderate — Serves 4 to 5

1/2 teaspoon salt

2 tablespoons Dijon mustard

1 1/2 teaspoons minced fresh
   rosemary, thyme or oregano

2 tablespoons fresh lemon juice

1/4 cup olive oil or peanut oil

2 racks of lamb

1/2 cup crustless fresh white
   bread crumbs

2 tablespoons butter, melted

Combine the salt, mustard, rosemary, lemon juice and olive oil in a small bowl and mix well. Score the fat on the bottom (bone side) of the lamb lightly with shallow crisscross marks. Spread the mustard mixture over the top and sides of the lamb. Wrap the bones with a double layer of foil and place the lamb in a roasting pan. Roast at 500 degrees on the upper middle oven rack for 10 minutes or until seared. Remove the lamb from the oven. Reduce the oven temperature to 400 degrees. Coat the top and sides of the lamb with the bread crumbs and drizzle the butter over the top. Return to the oven and roast for 20 minutes or until a meat thermometer registers 145 degrees for medium-rare. Let the lamb rest for 5 minutes before carving.

Photograph for this recipe appears on page 165.

A Thyme to Entertain

Green Beans with Roquefort and Walnuts

Moderate — Serves 4

Boil the green beans in water to cover in a saucepan for 3 to 4 minutes or until tender-crisp; drain. Rinse with cold water until cooled; drain and set aside. Cook the bacon in a skillet over medium heat for 5 to 7 minutes or until cooked through and crisp. Remove the bacon to paper towels to drain, reserving the drippings in the skillet. Add the green beans to the bacon drippings and sauté for 2 minutes or until heated through. Sprinkle with the cheese. Cook for 30 to 45 seconds or just until the cheese begins to melt, stirring constantly. Spoon into a serving bowl. Crumble the bacon. Sprinkle the green beans evenly with the bacon, walnuts, salt and pepper. Serve immediately.

Photograph of this recipe appears on page 165.

1 pound green beans, trimmed

4 slices thick-cut bacon

4 ounces Roquefort cheese, crumbled

1 cup walnuts, toasted

1/2 teaspoon salt

1/2 teaspoon pepper

Pumpkin Flan

Gourmet — Serves 8

1 cup sugar

2 1/2 cups skim milk

1 cup canned pumpkin purée

3 eggs

3 egg whites

1 teaspoon cinnamon

1 teaspoon vanilla extract

1/4 cup flaked coconut

Sprinkle 1/2 cup of the sugar in a 9-inch baking pan. Hold the pan over medium-high heat, wearing oven mitts. Cook until the sugar melts and caramelizes to a light golden brown, shaking the pan occasionally. Let stand until cool. (The mixture may crack slightly.) Combine the remaining 1/2 cup sugar and the milk in a saucepan and cook until hot and frothy, stirring constantly.

Beat the pumpkin, eggs, egg whites, cinnamon and vanilla on medium speed in a mixing bowl until blended. Add the hot milk mixture gradually, beating at low speed until incorporated. Pour the pumpkin mixture over the caramelized sugar. Place the baking pan in a larger baking pan. Pour hot water into the larger pan to a depth of 1 inch. Bake at 350 degrees for 1 hour or until a knife inserted in the center comes out clean. Remove the baking pan from the water and cool completely on a wire rack. Chill, covered, until set.

Spread the coconut on a rimmed baking sheet. Bake at 350 degrees for 5 to 6 minutes or until toasted, stirring occasionally. Remove from the oven and cool completely. Loosen the edge of the flan with a spatula and invert onto a serving plate. Sprinkle with the toasted coconut.

Egg Soufflé

Easy — Serves 6 to 8

Place the cheese spread and butter in a microwave-safe dish. Microwave on High at 30-second intervals until melted and smooth, stirring after each interval. Fold in the bread. Spread the bread mixture into a greased 9x13-inch glass or ceramic baking dish. Beat the eggs, milk, dry mustard and salt in a mixing bowl until frothy and pour over the bread. Break up the bread with a fork. Chill, covered, in the refrigerator for 8 to 10 hours. Remove from the refrigerator 1 hour prior to baking. Sprinkle the top with pimento. Bake at 300 degrees for 1 hour. Remove from the oven and cut into squares to serve. (Note: The soufflé will fall when removed from the oven.)

2 (5-ounce) jars Old English
    cheese spread
1/2 cup (1 stick) butter
12 slices white bread, trimmed
    and cut into quarters
6 eggs
2 cups milk
1/2 teaspoon dry mustard
1/2 teaspoon salt
Drained chopped pimento

Quiche à la Hanneke

Moderate — Serves 4 to 6

Roll out the puff pastry and fit into a greased quiche dish. Cover the bottom with a thin layer of the bread crumbs. Arrange the broccoli and ham evenly on top of the bread crumbs. Beat the eggs in a mixing bowl until slightly frothy. Mix in the crème fraîche, cheese, salt and pepper. Pour over the broccoli and ham, evenly distributing the cheese. Bake at 375 degrees on the middle oven rack for 35 to 40 minutes or until cooked through and set. (Note: For variations, try the ham with chopped mushrooms and chopped leeks, crumbled bacon with leeks or just crumbled bacon and cheese.)

1 sheet frozen puff pastry, thawed
1 to 2 tablespoons (about)
    bread crumbs
1 pound (or more) broccoli, chopped
    and cooked
8 ounces sliced ham, chopped
3 eggs
4 1/2 ounces crème fraîche
8 ounces Cheddar cheese, shredded
Salt and pepper to taste

Beef Stew with Mushrooms and Red Wine

Moderate — Serves 4 to 6

2¹/2 pounds boneless beef chuck,
    cut into 1¹/2-inch cubes

Salt and pepper to taste

All-purpose flour for coating

3 tablespoons (or more) vegetable oil

1 garlic clove, minced

2 cups dry red wine

3/4 cup (or more) beef stock

3 sprigs (or more) of fresh parsley

1 bay leaf

2 slices bacon

1 cup coarsely chopped onion

1 tablespoon tomato paste

1 pound mushrooms, cut into quarters

2 tablespoons butter, melted

Chopped fresh parsley

Season the beef with salt and pepper. Dredge in the flour, coating completely. Brown in batches in the hot oil in a Dutch oven for 5 minutes, adding more oil as needed and stirring to keep the cubes separate. Return all the beef to the Dutch oven. Add the garlic and cook for 1 minute. Stir in the wine and enough stock to cover the beef. Add the sprigs of parsley and bay leaf. Bake, covered, at 325 degrees for 2 hours.

Cook the bacon in a skillet until cooked through and crisp; drain, reserving the drippings in the skillet. Crumble the bacon. Add the onion to the skillet and sauté in the bacon drippings until translucent. Add the tomato paste and cook for 2 minutes, stirring constantly. Stir the onion mixture and bacon into the stew. Add more stock if needed to cover the beef. Bake, covered, for 30 minutes. Sauté the mushrooms in the butter in the skillet over high heat for 10 minutes or until tender. Add the mushrooms to the stew. Season the stew with salt and pepper. Chill, covered, in the refrigerator. To serve, bake at 325 degrees for 30 to 40 minutes or until heated through. Discard the bay leaf. Garnish with chopped fresh parsley.

State Circle Chicken

Easy — Serves 4

Brown the chicken in the butter and hot oil in a deep cast-iron skillet for 2 to 3 minutes on each side. Remove the chicken, reserving the drippings in the skillet. Add the mushrooms to the reserved drippings and sauté for 5 minutes. Return the chicken to the skillet. Stir in the soup, wine and water. Bring to a simmer and simmer for 10 minutes or until the chicken is cooked through. Combine the cream, salt, tarragon and pepper in a bowl and mix well. Pour over the chicken. Stir in the artichokes. Bake at 350 degrees for 35 minutes. Stir in the green onions and bake for 10 minutes longer. (Note: You may use your favorite chicken pieces instead of a whole chicken.)

1 whole chicken, cut up

1/4 cup (1/2 stick) butter, melted

1 tablespoon vegetable oil

8 ounces sliced mushrooms

1 (10-ounce) can cream of
    chicken soup

1 cup dry white wine

1 cup water

1/2 cup heavy cream or
    whipping cream

1 teaspoon salt

1/2 teaspoon tarragon

1/4 teaspoon pepper

1 (14-ounce) can artichokes, drained
    and chopped

6 green onions, finely chopped

Capital Carrots

Easy — Serves 6 to 8

2 pounds peeled carrots

Salt to taste

1/2 cup mayonnaise

1 tablespoon horseradish

1 tablespoon minced onion

Pepper to taste

1/4 cup fine bread crumbs

2 tablespoons margarine, softened

Paprika to taste

Chopped fresh parsley

Cook the carrots in boiling salted water in a large saucepan until tender. Drain, reserving 1/4 cup of the cooking liquid. Cut the carrots into halves lengthwise and arrange in a shallow baking dish. Combine the reserved cooking liquid, mayonnaise, horseradish and onion in a bowl and mix well. Season with pepper. Pour over the carrots. Sprinkle with the bread crumbs. Dot the top with the margarine and sprinkle with paprika and parsley. Bake at 350 degrees for 20 minutes. (Note: This recipe may be prepared in advance.)

The "Slaughter Across the Water" is an annual call to demonstrate civic pride and community morale. This event is held the first Saturday of November between rivals Downtown Annapolis and the Maritime Republic of Eastport and is the longest tug-of-war over a body of water in the world. It features a 1,700-foot-long rope with over 350 tuggers and thousands of spectators. It has raised over $185,000 for local charities since it started in 1997.

Tequila Cream Corn

Moderate — Serves 4 to 6

Sauté the shallot and garlic in the butter in a large skillet over medium heat for 1 minute or until tender. Add the corn and bell pepper and cook over medium heat for 4 minutes or until tender. Add the cream and tequila. Cook for 3 to 4 minutes or until slightly thickened, stirring constantly. (The corn may be made ahead up to this point and chilled in the refrigerator for up to 4 hours.) Just before serving, reheat the corn and stir in the scallions, cilantro, lime juice and kosher salt.

1 tablespoon minced shallot

1 tablespoon minced garlic

1 tablespoon unsalted butter, melted

2 1/2 cups frozen corn kernels

1/2 small red bell pepper,
   finely chopped

1/4 cup heavy cream

2 tablespoons tequila

1/2 cup thinly sliced scallions

1/4 cup finely chopped fresh cilantro

1 tablespoon fresh lime juice

Kosher salt to taste

Apple-Baked Sweet Potatoes

Moderate — Serves 6 to 8

Place the sweet potatoes in a large saucepan and cover with water. Bring to a boil and boil until tender; do not overcook. Drain and cool completely. Combine 1/2 cup brown sugar, the cinnamon and nutmeg in a bowl and mix well. Peel the sweet potatoes and slice into 1/4-inch-thick rounds. Peel, core and slice the apples into 1/4-inch-thick rings. Layer one-half of the sweet potatoes in a lightly greased 7x11-inch baking dish. Top with the apples, brown sugar mixture and remaining sweet potatoes. Combine the flour, 1/4 cup brown sugar, the butter and pecans in a bowl and mix well. Sprinkle over the sweet potatoes. Bake at 350 degrees for 30 minutes.

3 sweet potatoes

1/2 cup packed brown sugar

1 teaspoon cinnamon

1 teaspoon nutmeg

2 large Winesap apples or other
   baking apples

1/4 cup all-purpose flour

1/4 cup packed brown sugar

1/4 cup (1/2 stick) butter or
   margarine, softened

1/4 cup chopped pecans

Cheddar Cheese Bread Pudding

Moderate — Serves 6 to 8

6 tablespoons unsalted butter

6 slices homestyle white bread, crusts removed

1 1/2 cups milk

3 eggs

1 teaspoon salt

1/8 teaspoon Tabasco sauce

1 pound aged sharp Cheddar cheese, shredded

Butter a 1 1/2-quart soufflé dish with 1 tablespoon of the butter. Spread the remaining 5 tablespoons butter on one side of each slice of bread. Cut each slice of bread into thirds. Beat the milk, eggs, salt and Tabasco sauce in a mixing bowl until combined. Layer half the bread buttered side up and half the cheese in the prepared dish. Repeat the layers. Pour the egg mixture over the top. Chill, covered, for 45 minutes. Bake at 350 degrees for 40 to 45 minutes or until bubbly and golden brown. Serve immediately.

Walnut Streusel Apple Pie

Gourmet — Serves 8 to 10

Pastry

1 1/4 cups all-purpose flour

2 1/2 tablespoons sugar

1/2 teaspoon cinnamon

1/4 teaspoon salt

3 tablespoons unsalted butter, chilled and cut into small pieces

3 tablespoons unsalted margarine, chilled and cut into small pieces

1 1/2 teaspoons fresh lemon juice

2 to 4 tablespoons ice water

To prepare the pastry, combine the flour, sugar, cinnamon and salt in a food processor and process until combined. Add the butter and margarine and pulse until crumbly. Add the lemon juice, processing constantly until incorporated. Add the ice water gradually, processing constantly until the dough comes together in a ball. Chill, wrapped in waxed paper, for 4 to 10 hours. Roll into a 12-inch circle on a lightly floured surface. Fit into a 9- or 10-inch pie plate and flute or crimp the edge.

A Thyme to Entertain

To prepare the filling, combine the apples, raisins and ginger in a bowl and toss to combine. Arrange the apple mixture evenly in the pastry-lined pie plate. Combine the sour cream, egg, brown sugar, granulated sugar, flour, cinnamon and vanilla in a bowl and mix until smooth. Pour over the apple mixture. Bake at 400 degrees for 25 minutes. Remove the pie from the oven and reduce the oven temperature to 350 degrees.

To prepare the streusel, combine the brown sugar, flour and walnuts in a bowl and stir until combined. Cut in the butter until crumbly and sprinkle on top of the pie. Bake for 45 minutes.

Filling

5 tart apples, peeled and sliced

1 cup golden raisins

2 tablespoons minced candied ginger

1 cup sour cream

1 egg, beaten

1/3 cup packed brown sugar

1/3 granulated sugar

3 tablespoons all-purpose flour

2 teaspoons cinnamon

1 teaspoon vanilla extract

Streusel

3/4 cup packed brown sugar

1/2 cup all-purpose flour

3 tablespoons chopped
  walnuts, toasted

1/3 cup butter, chilled and
  cut into small pieces

For an autumn party, write each guest's name on a pretty leaf and use it as a place card at each place setting.

HOLIDAY GATHERING

The holiday gathering has been a celebrated event in Annapolis history since the 17TH century. You can always find friends and families enjoying each other's company. The Menorahs and Christmas trees are lit to honor this special season. The snow is gently falling; the rivers are still and quiet. We hope that you enjoy outdoor festivities, peaceful evenings by the fire, holiday celebrations and don't forget to invite many friends.

Holiday Gathering

Pomegranate Martini

Cheddar Almond Strips

Confetti Spinach Salad

Peppercorn Tenderloin

Sesame Noodles with Asparagus

Coconut, Caramel and Rum Flan

...a celebration in Annapolis since the 17th century

Pomegranate Martini

Easy — Serves 4

2 cups pomegranate juice

4 ounces citrus-flavored vodka

2 ounces Triple Sec

1/2 ounce fresh lemon juice

Pomegranate seeds

Chill the pomegranate juice, vodka, Triple Sec and lemon juice. Combine the chilled ingredients in a martini pitcher and mix well. Pour into four chilled martini glasses and garnish with pomegranate seeds.

Cheddar Almond Strips

Easy — Serves 10 to 12

1 (1-pound) loaf sliced white bread

8 ounces Cheddar cheese, shredded

6 slices bacon, crisp-cooked
   and crumbled

1 small onion, finely chopped

1 cup mayonnaise

1 tablespoon Worcestershire sauce

1 (2-ounce) package slivered almonds

Salt and pepper to taste

Cut the crust from the bread and discard. Cut each bread slice into four even strips. Combine the cheese, bacon, onion, mayonnaise, Worcestershire sauce and almonds in a bowl and stir until combined. Spread the cheese mixture on the strips of bread and place on a baking sheet. Bake at 400 degrees for 10 minutes. Serve warm or at room temperature. (Note: The Cheddar Almond Strips may be frozen prior to baking.)

A Thyme to Entertain

Confetti Spinach Salad

Easy — Serves 6 to 8

Chop the apples and place in a large salad bowl. Add 2 tablespoons lemon juice and toss to coat. Add the spinach and dried cranberries. Whisk 2 tablespoons lemon juice, the olive oil, vinegar, honey, salt and pepper in a small bowl until the olive oil is incorporated. Pour the vinaigrette over the spinach mixture and toss until well coated. Sprinkle with the goat cheese and walnuts.

2 Red Delicious apples

2 tablespoons lemon juice

8 cups baby spinach leaves

1/2 cup dried cranberries

2 tablespoons lemon juice

3 tablespoons olive oil

1 tablespoon apple cider vinegar

2 tablespoons honey

Salt and pepper to taste

2/3 cup crumbled goat cheese

1/2 cup chopped walnuts, toasted

Annapolis by Candlelight takes you back to the eighteenth century when our founding fathers walked our quaint streets. In early November you can join the Annapolis Historical Foundation on guided candlelight tours through privately owned historic homes. Your tour will be led by a curator dressed in period costume. This autumn experience gives you a glimpse of old-world Annapolis, culture, and architecture.

Sponsored by

Peppercorn Tenderloin

Moderate — Serves 6 to 8

1 (3- to 4-pound) beef tenderloin

3 tablespoons Dijon mustard

1 1/2 tablespoons drained
  green peppercorns

1 tablespoon coarsely ground
  5-peppercorn blend
  (*see* note below)

8 large fresh sage leaves

2 tablespoons unsalted
  butter, softened

2 tablespoons coarsely ground
  5-peppercorn blend
  (*see* note below)

Salt to taste

4 bay leaves

Slice the beef lengthwise through two-thirds of the thickness. Spread the beef out and flatten slightly with a meat pounder. Spread the mustard in a thin layer over the cut open side of the beef. Sprinkle with the green peppercorns and slightly press the green peppercorns into the beef. Sprinkle with 1 tablespoon 5-peppercorn blend. Place the sage leaves in a row down the vertical center of the beef. Roll the beef into its original shape and secure with kitchen twine at four evenly spaced places. Rub the outside of the beef with the butter and press 2 tablespoons 5-peppercorn blend into the buttered surface of the beef. Season with salt.

Arrange the beef seam side down in a shallow roasting pan. Slide a bay leave under each of the butcher's twine ties on the top of the beef. Bake at 425 degrees for 45 to 55 minutes. Let stand for 10 minutes before carving. Discard the bay leaves. Cut away the butcher's twine and slice the beef. Serve with the pan drippings spooned on top. (Note: To prepare the 5-peppercorn blend, mix equal parts of green peppercorns, black peppercorns, white peppercorns, pink peppercorns and whole allspice in a peppermill.)

Photograph for this recipe appears on page 181.

Sesame Noodles with Asparagus

Easy — Serves 6 to 8

Whisk the soy sauce, sesame oil, brown sugar, dark sesame oil, vinegar and chili oil in a bowl until the sugar dissolves. Whisk in the cilantro, ginger, garlic and 2 teaspoons salt. Cook the asparagus in boiling salted water in a large saucepan until tender-crisp; drain and dry on a kitchen towel. Cook the pasta in boiling salted water in the saucepan until cooked through; drain and place in a serving bowl. Reserve some of the asparagus pieces, some of the scallions and some of the sesame seeds. Add the remaining asparagus, scallions and sesame seeds to the pasta. Add the sauce and toss until well coated. Sprinkle the reserved asparagus, scallions and sesame seeds over the top. Serve warm or at room temperature.

7 tablespoons soy sauce

1/4 cup sesame oil

31/2 tablespoons dark brown sugar

3 tablespoons dark sesame oil

3 tablespoons balsamic vinegar

2 teaspoons chili oil

1/4 cup chopped cilantro

1 tablespoon minced fresh ginger

1 garlic clove, minced

2 teaspoons salt

2 pounds asparagus, trimmed and
    thinly sliced on the diagonal

Salt to taste

16 ounces angel hair pasta

10 scallions, thinly sliced

1/4 cup sesame seeds, lightly toasted

Coconut, Caramel and Rum Flan

Easy — Serves 6

6 egg yolks

1 cup canned unsweetened
   coconut milk

1 cup whipping cream

1/2 cup sugar

1/4 cup caramel topping

2 tablespoons dark rum

1 teaspoon vanilla extract

Pinch of salt

1/2 cup sweetened flaked
   coconut, toasted

Combine the egg yolks, coconut milk, cream, sugar, caramel topping, rum, vanilla and salt in a bowl and whisk until smooth. Pour into a 2-quart terrine. Place the terrine in a 9x13-inch metal baking pan. Add enough hot water to the baking pan to come half-way up the sides of the terrine. Bake at 350 degrees for 1 hour or until set and golden brown. Remove the terrine from the water and chill, uncovered, until cold. Cover and chill for 3 hours longer. Loosen the edge of the flan with a spatula and invert onto a serving plate. Sprinkle with the toasted coconut. (Note: You may prepare this recipe up to 1 day in advance. This recipe can be doubled easily.)

Bundle up for a fun evening of boats, lights, and holiday cheer. The Parade of Lights is an Annapolis tradition that dates back to 1981. Jim Langer, a Spa Creek resident, decided to decorate his floating home and parade through City Dock. This solo man founded the event now known as the official Maryland Winter Celebration. Annapolitans decorate boats of all sizes to entertain people who have traveled from near and far. The boats parade from Spa Creek to Annapolis City Dock. Gather your friends and family together, grab a hot drink from one of the local coffee houses, and enjoy the festivities.

Santa's Punch

Easy — Serves 2 to 4

Combine the rum, schnapps, amaretto, cranberry juice and lemon-lime soda in a pitcher. Serve over ice in drinking glasses or punch glasses.

1 ounce light rum

1 ounce peach schnapps

1 ounce amaretto

1^1/$_2$ cups cranberry juice

1 cup lemon-lime soda

Cherry Brandy Sours

Easy — Serves 2 to 4

Combine the lemonade concentrate, orange juice concentrate and brandy in a blender. Add the ice and process until smooth.

1 (6-ounce) can frozen
    lemonade concentrate

1 (6-ounce) can frozen orange
    juice concentrate

6 ounces cherry-flavored brandy

1 tray of ice cubes

Cheese Grits

Easy — Serves 10 to 12

1 (24-ounce) container grits

1/2 cup (1 stick) butter, cut into pieces

1 cup (4 ounces) shredded
   Cheddar cheese

2 eggs

1/2 cup (about) milk

1 cup (4 ounces) shredded
   Parmesan cheese

Dash of paprika

Salt and pepper to taste

Prepare enough grits to serve ten to twelve people according to the package directions. Add the butter and Cheddar cheese to the warm grits and stir until melted. Let stand until cool. Break the eggs into a 1-cup liquid measuring cup and add milk to measure 1 cup. Add to the cooled grits mixture and stir until well blended. Spoon into a 3-quart baking dish. Sprinkle the parmesan cheese evenly over the grits mixture. Sprinkle the paprika on top. Bake at 375 degrees for 35 to 40 minutes or until heated through. Serve warm.

French Toast Soufflé

Easy — Serves 8 to 10

10 cups (1-inch) cubes hearty white
   bread (about 16 slices)

8 ounces cream cheese, softened

8 eggs

1 1/2 cups 2% milk

2/3 cup half-and-half

1/2 cup pure maple syrup

1/2 teaspoon vanilla extract

Pure maple syrup

Confectioners' sugar

Cinnamon

Arrange the bread evenly in a greased 9x13-inch baking pan. Beat the cream cheese in a mixing bowl until smooth. Add the eggs one at a time, mixing well after each addition. Add the milk, half-and-half, 1/2 cup maple syrup and the vanilla and beat until smooth. Pour evenly over the bread. Chill, covered, for 8 to 10 hours. Let stand at room temperature for 30 minutes prior to baking. Bake at 375 degrees for 50 minutes or until set. Drizzle with maple syrup and sprinkle with confectioners' sugar and cinnamon. Serve immediately.

Christmas Morning Eggs

Easy — Serves 6 to 8

Arrange eight slices of the bread in a greased 9x13-inch baking pan. Top with the ham, cheese and remaining eight bread slices. Beat the eggs, salt and pepper in a mixing bowl. Add the dry mustard, onion, bell pepper, Worcestershire sauce, milk and Tabasco sauce and beat until combined. Pour over the layers. Chill, covered, in the refrigerator for 8 to 10 hours. Combine the butter and cereal in a bowl and mix well. Cover the casserole completely with the cereal mixture. Bake at 350 degrees for 1 hour or until the center is set and the sides are bubbly.

16 slices white sandwich bread, crusts removed

1 ham steak, cut into cubes

10 ounces sharp Cheddar cheese, shredded

6 eggs

1/2 teaspoon salt

1/2 teaspoon pepper

1/2 to 1 teaspoon dry mustard

1/4 cup minced onion

1/4 cup finely chopped green bell pepper

1 to 2 teaspoons Worcestershire sauce

3 cups milk

Dash of Tabasco sauce

1/2 cup (1 stick) butter, melted

2 cups crushed cornflakes

There are approximately 160 active members of The Junior League of Annapolis who contribute over 20,000 hours of volunteer time in any given year. These women of diverse backgrounds are artists, architects, businesswomen, engineers, attorneys, wives, and mothers who wish to make lasting contributions to the community outside of their chosen vocation.

Sponsored by

Greeley and Hurley McDermott
in loving memory of Stella Hurley, 1906-2007

Chicken Divan

Easy — Serves 8

8 chicken breasts

1 teaspoon salt

2 (10-ounce) packages frozen
  broccoli spears

1 (10-ounce) can cream of
  chicken soup

3/4 cup sour cream

1/2 cup mayonnaise

2 tablespoons dry sherry

1 teaspoon mustard

1/4 teaspoon curry powder

1/3 cup grated Parmesan cheese

1 (6-ounce) package wild rice, or
  8 ounces vermicelli, cooked

Paprika to taste

Combine the chicken and salt with water to cover in a large heavy saucepan. Bring to a boil and then reduce the heat. Simmer, covered, for 1 hour or until the chicken is cooked through. Drain the chicken and let stand until cool. Coarsely chop the chicken, discarding the skin and bones. Cook the broccoli according to the package directions; drain. Combine the soup, sour cream, mayonnaise, sherry, mustard, curry powder and cheese in a bowl and mix until combined. Layer the wild rice, broccoli, half of the soup mixture, chicken and remaining soup mixture in a lightly greased 9x13-inch baking dish. Chill, covered, for 8 to 10 hours. Let stand at room temperature for 30 minutes prior to baking. Bake at 350 degrees for 45 minutes. Sprinkle with paprika before serving.

A Thyme to Entertain

Pork with Sherry Portobello Sauce

Easy — Serves 4 to 6

To prepare the pork, combine the olive oil, vinegar, marjoram, salt and pepper in a bowl and mix until incorporated. Pour into an extra-large sealable plastic bag and add the pork. Seal the bag and turn several times to coat. Marinate in the refrigerator for 2 to 24 hours. Drain the pork, reserving the marinade. Place the pork on a grill rack and grill until cooked through, turning occasionally and brushing with the reserved marinade.

To prepare the sauce, sauté the leek and garlic in the butter in a large skillet for 3 to 4 minutes or until the leek is tender. Add the portobellos and sauté for 3 to 4 minutes or until the mushrooms are tender. Stir in the sherry, mustard and Worcestershire sauce and cook for 1 to 2 minutes or until the sauce begins to boil. Reduce the heat to medium-low and stir in the sour cream, salt and white pepper. To serve, slice the pork and serve with the sauce spooned on top. (Note: Instead of grilling, you may roast the pork at 400 degrees in a shallow roasting pan for 1 hour or until cooked through, turning occasionally and brushing with the reserved marinade.)

Pork

1/4 cup olive oil

2 tablespoons white wine vinegar

2 tablespoons chopped fresh
    marjoram, or 2 teaspoons
    dried marjoram

1/2 teaspoon salt

1/4 teaspoon pepper

3 (12-ounce) pork tenderloins

Sherry Portobello Sauce

1/2 leek, cut into halves lengthwise
    and sliced

2 garlic cloves, minced

2 tablespoons butter, melted

2 cups sliced portobellos

2 tablespoons dry sherry

1 tablespoon Dijon mustard

2 teaspoons Worcestershire sauce

1 cup sour cream

1/4 teaspoon salt

1/8 teaspoon white pepper

Heavenly Onions

Easy — Serves 8 to 10

6 large Vidalia onions, cut into
    1/4-inch slices

6 tablespoons butter, melted

1 pound Swiss cheese, shredded

1/2 teaspoon pepper

1 (10-ounce) can cream of
    chicken soup

1 cup cream

2 teaspoons soy sauce

Butter for the bread

8 slices French bread

Sauté the onions in 6 tablespoons butter in a skillet until tender. Spoon into a 9x13-inch baking dish. Sprinkle the cheese and pepper evenly over the onions. Combine the soup, cream and soy sauce in a bowl and mix until smooth. Spoon evenly over the cheese layer. Butter one side of each slice of bread and place on top of the soup mixture butter side up. Bake at 350 degrees for 30 minutes.

Praline Sauce

Easy — Serves 6 to 8

1 1/4 cups packed brown sugar

1 (5-ounce) can evaporated milk

1 tablespoon butter

1/2 teaspoon rum, or to taste

1/3 cup chopped pecans

Good-quality vanilla ice cream

Combine the brown sugar, evaporated milk and butter in a saucepan and cook until smooth and syrupy, stirring occasionally. Stir in the rum and pecans. Serve warm over ice cream.

A Thyme to Entertain

Baklava

Gourmet — Serves 20 or more

Unroll the phyllo dough and cut the stack into halves. Cover with waxed paper topped with a damp towel. Keep the unused portion covered until needed. Combine the nuts and cinnamon in a bowl and mix well. Layer two sheets of phyllo dough in a buttered 9x13-inch baking dish, brushing the top sheet generously with butter. Sprinkle 2 to 3 tablespoons of the nut mixture over the top. Repeat the layers until six sheets of the phyllo dough remain.

Cut the baklava into diamond shapes, cutting through all the layers. Bake at 350 degrees for 1 hour or until golden brown and crisp. Bring the sugar and water to a boil in a saucepan over medium heat. Stir in the honey, vanilla and lemon zest and reduce the heat to a simmer. Simmer for 20 minutes. Remove the baklava from the oven and immediately spoon the syrup over the top. Let stand until completely cool. Store uncovered.

1 (16-ounce) package phyllo dough

1 pound chopped mixed nuts

1 teaspoon cinnamon

1 cup (2 sticks) butter, melted

1 cup sugar

1 cup water

1/2 cup honey

1 teaspoon vanilla extract

1 teaspoon grated lemon zest

The Junior League of Annapolis, Inc. was recognized nationally when then President Susan Neely was invited to the White House to attend a luncheon hosted by First Lady Barbara Bush. While there she received the National Volunteer Recognition Award for the Tommy Tummy project, which taught school children about the dangers of toxic substances.

Peaches and Cream Cake

Gourmet — Serves 12

Cake

3 cups soft wheat flour

1 teaspoon baking powder

1/2 teaspoon baking soda

1 teaspoon salt

1 cup (2 sticks) unsalted
     butter, softened

2 cups sugar

6 eggs

1 cup buttermilk

2 teaspoons vanilla extract

Meringue

1 to 2 teaspoons sugar

1 cup chopped pecans, toasted

3/4 cup sugar

4 egg whites, at room temperature

1/8 teaspoon cream of tartar

Pinch of salt

To prepare the cake, mix the wheat flour, baking powder, baking soda and salt together. Beat the butter at medium speed in a mixing bowl until creamy. Add the sugar gradually, beating constantly until light and fluffy. Add the eggs one at a time, beating until combined after each addition. Add the flour mixture alternately with the buttermilk, beating at low speed until combined after each addition and beginning and ending with the flour mixture. Stir in the vanilla. Pour into two greased and floured 10-inch cake pans or springform pans. Bake at 325 degrees for 30 to 35 minutes or until wooden picks inserted in the centers come out clean. Cool the layers in the pans on wire racks for 10 minutes. Remove from the pans and cool completely on wire racks.

To prepare the meringue, grease a 10-inch springform pan and line the bottom with foil. Grease the foil and sprinkle the foil and side of the pan with 1 to 2 teaspoons sugar. Process the pecans and 3/4 cup sugar in a food processor fitted with the knife blade until the pecans are ground, stopping once to scrape down the side. Beat the egg whites, cream of tartar and salt at high speed in a mixing bowl until soft peaks form. Fold in the pecan mixture and spread in the prepared pan. Bake at 250 degrees for 1 1/2 to 1 3/4 hours or until thoroughly dry. Cool completely in the pan on a wire rack. Remove from the pan.

To prepare the peach filling, bring the peaches and water to a boil in a saucepan over medium heat. Cover and remove from the heat. Let stand for 30 minutes or until the peaches are soft. Stir in the sugar and corn syrup. Bring to a boil and then reduce the heat. Simmer for 30 minutes or until most of the liquid evaporates. Remove from the heat. Process the peach mixture in a food processor fitted with a knife blade until smooth, stopping once to scrape down the side. Let stand until cool.

To prepare the frosting, beat the butter, 1 cup of the confectioners' sugar and the flavorings at medium speed in a mixing bowl until combined. Add the remaining confectioners' sugar alternately with the cream, beating well after each addition. Beat at high speed until smooth and of a spreading consistency.

To assemble, place one of the cake layers on a cake plate and spread with one-half of the peach filling. Spread 1 cup of the frosting over the filling and top with the meringue layer. Spread the remaining peach filling over the meringue layer. Spread 1 1/2 cups of the remaining frosting over the peach filling. Top with the remaining cake layer. Spread the top and side of the cake with the remaining frosting. Chill for 2 to 3 hours before serving.

Peach Filling

1 3/4 cups dried peaches

1 1/2 cups water

1/4 cup sugar

2 tablespoons light corn syrup

Butter Whip Frosting

1 1/4 cups (2 1/2 sticks) unsalted
    butter, softened

2 (16-ounce) packages confectioners'
    sugar, sifted

2 teaspoons vanilla extract

1/4 teaspoon almond extract

1 1/2 cups whipping cream

A Sweet Ending

Nana's Anise Cookies

Amaretto Truffles · Cranberry Nut Torte

Poached Pears with Raspberry Sauce

Raspberry White Chocolate Tiramisu

Cracker Candies

...a peaceful evening by the fire

Nana's Anise Cookies

Easy — Makes 2 to 4 dozen

5 cups all-purpose flour

2 tablespoons baking powder

1 cup (2 sticks) salted butter, softened

1 cup granulated sugar

6 eggs

2 teaspoons vanilla extract

4 teaspoons anise extract

1/2 cup confectioners' sugar

1 teaspoon anise extract

Water, as needed

Nonpareils (optional)

Mix the flour and baking powder in a bowl and set aside. Cream the butter and granulated sugar in a mixing bowl until light and fluffy. Beat in the eggs, vanilla and 4 teaspoons anise extract. Add the flour mixture in thirds, mixing well after each addition. Roll by spoonfuls into desired shapes with floured hands and place on a greased cookie sheet. (Shapes such as stars, hearts, pinwheels, S's and C's work well.) Bake at 350 degrees for 10 minutes or until light brown. Remove from the oven and cool on a wire rack. Combine the confectioners' sugar and 1 teaspoon anise extract in a bowl and mix well. Stir in enough water to form a smooth icing consistency. Dip the cookies in the icing and immediately into nonpareils. Let stand until firm. (Note: These cookies pair well with coffee.)

A Thyme to Entertain

Amaretto Truffles

Easy — Makes 2 dozen

3 cups (18 ounces) semisweet
    chocolate chips
1 (14-ounce) can sweetened
    condensed milk
3 tablespoons amaretto
1/2 teaspoon almond extract
Finely chopped almonds

Place the chocolate chips and sweetened condensed milk in a microwave-safe bowl. Microwave on High at 30-second intervals until melted and smooth, stirring after each interval. Stir in the liqueur and almond extract. Chill, covered, for 2 hours. Roll the chocolate mixture into 1-inch balls and then roll in almonds, coating completely.

Photograph for this recipe appears on page 197.

In order to fund volunteer training, league administration, and projects, The Junior League of Annapolis has organized a number of successful fund-raisers over the past quarter century including tag sales, auction galas, and a cookbook, Of Tide and Thyme. Of Tide and Thyme *is currently in its tenth printing and more than 70,000 copies have been sold locally and by major booksellers throughout the United States.*

Cranberry Nut Torte
Moderate — Serves 8 to 10

To prepare the crust, process the walnuts in a food processor until finely ground. Combine the walnuts, sugar and butter in a bowl and mix well. Press the walnut mixture evenly over the bottom of an 8-inch springform pan.

To prepare the filling, combine the sugar, flour, butter, eggs and almond extract in a bowl and mix until combined. Process the walnuts and cranberries in a food processor until coarsely chopped and stir into the filling. Spread the filling evenly over the crust. Bake at 350 degrees for 1 hour. Let stand until cool. To serve, remove the side of the springform pan and dust the top of the torte with confectioners' sugar.

Photograph for this recipe appears on page 197.

Crust

2 cups walnuts

2 tablespoons sugar

2 tablespoons unsalted
    butter, melted

Filling

1 cup granulated sugar

3/4 cup all-purpose flour

1/2 cup (1 stick) unsalted
    butter, melted

2 eggs

1 1/2 teaspoons almond extract

1/2 cup walnuts

1 cup cranberries

Confectioners' sugar

Poached Pears with Raspberry Sauce

Gourmet — Serves 12

Poached Pears

2 cups water

1/3 cup lemon juice

12 pears

4 cups apple cider

2 cups dry white wine

1 cup sugar

Chocolate Truffle Filling

1 cup (6 ounces) semisweet
   chocolate chips

4 ounces cream cheese, softened

1 teaspoon vanilla extract

Raspberry Sauce

2 (10-ounce) packages frozen
   raspberries in heavy
   syrup, thawed

2/3 cup white zinfandel

1/3 cup raspberry schnapps or other
   raspberry-flavored liqueur

To prepare the pears, combine the water and lemon juice in a bowl and mix well. Cut a thin slice off the bottom of the pears so they can stand upright; peel the pears with a vegetable peeler. Core the pears from the bottom, cutting to but not through the stem, leaving the stem intact. Dip the pears in the lemon juice mixture, coating well. Combine the apple cider, wine and sugar in a large heavy saucepan and bring to a boil, stirring occasionally. Add the pears standing upright. Cover and reduce the heat to a simmer. Simmer for 15 to 20 minutes or until the pears are tender. Remove the saucepan from the heat and let stand, leaving the pears in the cooking liquid until completely cool. Drain the pears, discarding the cooking liquid.

To prepare the filling, place the chocolate chips, cream cheese and vanilla in a microwave-safe bowl. Microwave on High at 30-second intervals until melted and smooth, stirring after each interval. Fill the cavity of the pears with the chocolate filling. Chill, covered, in the refrigerator. (This can be done up to 10 hours in advance.)

To prepare the sauce, place the raspberries in a blender and process until smooth. Strain into a bowl, discarding any solids. Stir in the wine and schnapps. Chill, covered, in the refrigerator. To serve, remove the pears from the refrigerator 2 hours prior to serving. Place the poached pears on dessert plates. Drizzle the chilled raspberry sauce around or over the pears.

A Thyme to Entertain

Raspberry White Chocolate Tiramisu

Moderate — Serves 12 to 15

12 ounces white chocolate,
   coarsely chopped

$1/4$ cup whipping cream

3 ounces cream cheese or
   mascarpone cheese, softened

$1^1/4$ cups heavy whipping cream

$1^1/4$ cups brewed espresso or
   strong coffee, cooled

2 tablespoons brandy

36 ladyfingers, cut into halves
   horizontally

1 pint raspberries

Place the white chocolate and $1/4$ cup whipping cream in the top of a double boiler over hot water. Cook until melted and smooth, stirring frequently. Let stand until cool. Beat the cream cheese in a mixing bowl until fluffy. Blend in the white chocolate mixture. Whip $1^1/4$ cups whipping cream in a mixing bowl until stiff peaks form. Fold gently into the white chocolate mixture. Combine the espresso and brandy in a bowl and mix well. Line the sides of a 9-inch springform pan with ladyfinger halves lined up vertically with the cut sides facing in. Layer one-half of the remaining ladyfingers cut side up in the bottom of the pan. Brush with some of the espresso mixture. Spoon one-half of the white chocolate mixture over the top. Cover with the remaining ladyfingers and brush with the espresso mixture. Spoon the remaining white chocolate mixture over the top. Arrange the raspberries on top. Chill, covered, in the refrigerator for 4 to 10 hours.

Photograph for this recipe appears on page 197.

Cracker Candies

Easy — Serves 10

Line a rimmed baking sheet with baking parchment. Arrange the crackers in a single layer on the prepared baking sheet to completely cover the baking sheet. Combine the sugar and butter in a saucepan and cook until melted and smooth, stirring frequently. Pour evenly over the crackers. Bake at 350 degrees for 12 to 14 minutes or until bubbly. Remove from the oven and sprinkle the chocolate chips, peanut butter chips, toffee chips, pecans and coconut evenly on top. Cover with a sheet of waxed paper and lightly press the toppings into the hot butter mixture. Chill in the refrigerator until firm. Remove the waxed paper and break the candy into pieces.

Photograph for this recipe appears on page 197.

1 sleeve saltine crackers

1 cup sugar

1 cup (2 sticks) butter

2 cups (12 ounces) milk chocolate chips

1 (10-ounce) package peanut butter chips

3/4 cup toffee chips

3/4 cup chopped pecans

3/4 cup shredded coconut (optional)

No-Bake Peanut Butter Bars

Easy — Makes 30 to 40

Combine the graham cracker crumbs, confectioners' sugar, peanut butter and butter in a bowl and mix well. Press into a 9x13-inch baking pan. Melt the chocolate chips and shortening in a saucepan over low heat until smooth, stirring constantly. Spread evenly over the peanut butter layer. Chill, covered, in the refrigerator for 20 minutes. Cut into squares.

11/2 to 13/4 cups graham cracker crumbs

11/2 cups confectioners' sugar

11/2 cups peanut butter

1/2 cup (1 stick) butter, melted

2 cups (12 ounces) semisweet chocolate chips

1 tablespoon shortening

Whiskey Cake

Moderate — Serves 10 to 12

1 (2 layer) package yellow cake mix

1 (4-ounce) package vanilla instant
    pudding mix

4 eggs, lightly beaten

1 cup milk

1/2 cup vegetable oil

1 shot whiskey

3/4 cup confectioners' sugar

1/2 cup (1 stick) butter, cut into pieces

1/4 cup whiskey

Combine the cake mix and pudding mix in a mixing bowl and mix well. Add the eggs, milk, oil and 1 shot whiskey and blend until smooth. Pour evenly into a greased and floured bundt pan. Bake according to the cake mix package directions. Let stand in the pan to cool slightly. Invert the cake onto a wire rack on top of a rimmed baking sheet. Combine the confectioners' sugar, butter and 1/4 cup whiskey in a saucepan. Cook over low heat until melted and smooth, stirring frequently. Poke many holes in the top of the cake with a wooden pick. Slowly pour the sauce over the top of the cake while poking additional holes. Continue spooning the unabsorbed sauce over the cake until all the sauce has been absorbed. Cover and let stand at room temperature before serving. (Note: The more holes that are poked in the cake, the better the sauce soaks in.)

A Thyme to Entertain

Cherries in the Snow

Easy — Serves 8

Beat the cream cheese and 1/3 cup confectioners' sugar in a mixing bowl until light and fluffy. Whip the whipping cream at medium speed in a mixing bowl with a wire whisk attachment until soft peaks form. Add 1/2 cup confectioners' sugar gradually, beating until incorporated after each addition. Add a small amount of additional confectioners' sugar if desired for sweeter whipped cream. Fold in the vanilla. Fold the whipped cream mixture into the cream cheese mixture until incorporated. Spread evenly in the pie shell. Spread the cherry pie filling evenly over the top. Chill, covered, in the refrigerator until ready to serve.

8 ounces cream cheese, softened

1/3 cup confectioners' sugar

2 cups heavy whipping cream

1/2 cup (or more) confectioners' sugar

1 teaspoon vanilla extract

1 (21-ounce) can cherry pie filling

1 (9-inch) graham cracker pie shell or shortbread pie shell

Chinese Noodle Cookies

Easy — Makes 3 1/2 dozen

Place the chocolate chips and butterscotch chips in the top of a double boiler. Cook over hot water until melted and smooth, stirring frequently. Stir in the peanuts and chow mein noodles. Drop by teaspoonfuls onto a waxed paper-lined baking sheet. Chill, covered, until firm. (Note: This recipe is fun to prepare with children.)

2 cups (12 ounces) semisweet chocolate chips

1 (11-ounce) package butterscotch chips

2 cups chopped salted peanuts

2 cups chow mein noodles

Chocolate Peanut Butter Tandy Squares

Easy — Makes 2 dozen

4 eggs

2 cups sugar

2 cups all-purpose flour

1 teaspoon vanilla extract

1 cup milk

2 tablespoons butter

1 (18-ounce) jar creamy
  peanut butter

2 large milk chocolate candy bars

2 tablespoons butter

Beat the eggs and sugar in a mixing bowl until well blended. Beat in the flour and vanilla. Scald the milk in a saucepan. Remove from the heat and add 2 tablespoons butter, stirring until melted. Pour the milk mixture gradually into the egg mixture, beating constantly. Pour the batter into a greased 10x15-inch cake pan. Bake at 350 degrees for 20 minutes. Remove from the oven and immediately spread the peanut butter evenly over the top. Let stand until completely cool. Melt the candy bars and 2 tablespoons butter in a small heavy saucepan over low heat, stirring constantly. Spread evenly over the peanut butter layer. Let stand until the chocolate is set and cut into squares.

Spiced Sugar Pecans

Easy — Makes 2¹/2 cups

Place the pecans in a single layer on a rimmed baking sheet or in a shallow baking pan. Bake at 375 degrees for 12 to 15 minutes or until toasted. Combine the sugar, water, cinnamon and salt in a saucepan and mix well. Cook, uncovered, over high heat to 234 to 240 degrees on a candy thermometer, soft-ball stage; do not stir. Remove from the heat. Stir in the vanilla and pecans gently until the pecans are completely coated and the mixture is creamy. Spread the mixture onto a greased baking pan, separating the pecan halves as they cool.

2¹/2 cups pecan halves

1 cup sugar

¹/2 cup water

1 teaspoon cinnamon

1 teaspoon salt

1 teaspoon vanilla extract

Crispy Peanut Butter Balls

Moderate — Makes 4 dozen

Combine the cereal, peanut butter, confectioners' sugar and butter in a bowl and mix well by hand. Roll the mixture into walnut-sized balls. Melt the chocolate candy melts according to the package directions. Dip the peanut butter balls into the melted chocolate, coating completely. Place on a sheet of waxed paper and air dry until firm.

3 cups crisp rice cereal

2 cups creamy peanut butter

1 (1-pound) package confectioners' sugar

¹/2 cup (1 stick) butter, melted

12 to 16 ounces chocolate candy melts

ABOUT THE PHOTOGRAPHER & FOOD STYLIST

THE PHOTOGRAPHER

Dean Alexander is a commercial photographer with twenty years of professional experience. His photography has received international recognition and numerous awards. He is well known regionally for his ability to partner with clients and create images that are artistic and original. His food photography in particular has been featured in *Bon Appétit* and *Art Culinaire*, among others. Dean resides in Baltimore with his wife and daughter.

THE FOOD STYLIST

Creativity and artistry are the key ingredients to food stylist Chef Stephanie Rose's work. Stephanie Rose learned her art during five years at The Television Food Network in New York City and apprenticed with top New York and Washington DC food stylists. Recent clients include former White House chef and author Walter Scheib, television barbecue personality Steven Raichlen, Cuisinart, and *The Washington Post*.

Prior to shifting into commercial food design, Chef Rose studied cuisine at the Institute of Culinary Education in New York City and at La Varenne Ecole de Cuisine in France. She also worked for leading chefs of America at Lespinasse and at the Watergate for the late Jean-Louis Palladin. This experience, plus several years as an event planner at the historic Puck Building in New York City, have honed Chef Rose's eye for visual impact.

ACKNOWLEDGMENTS

A special thank you to the following people for providing *A Thyme to Entertain* with donations of food, opening up their homes, or letting us borrow their beautiful decor and china to use as props for the photography.

© Annapolis and Anne Arundel County Conference and Visitors Bureau—Photography for pages 73, 119, 163, and 179

Cathal Armstrong/ Restaurant Eve—Donating mushrooms, herbs and produce

© The Baltimore Sun Company—Photography for pages 43, 59, 89, 103, 135, and 149

© Big Stock Photo—Photography for page 15

Wendy Bogarde—Props

Jane Bowen—Home

Robert Devita—Map Design

Kelly Dovi—Props

Kristin Walter Dukes/The Cairn—Props

Jan Duffy—Props

© Four Seasons Publishing, Inc.—Invitations for pages 16, 74, 136, 164, and 180

© Glad Tidings, Inc.—Invitation for page 120

Mike Gosnell—Cooked crabs

Stephanie Griffith—Props

Bennet Helfgott/M. Slavin & Sons Fish—Deal on seafood

Susan Crais Hovanec—Use of kitchen

KOOL Ice—Crabs

© Lovie and Dodge—Invitation for page 30

Dee Murray—Antique car prop

Bill Nalley—Antique car prop

Marc and Katherine Norgaard—Home

© Odd Balls—Invitations for pages 60, 104, 150, and 196

Parkemoor Home—Props

© Christie Pirrung Stationery—Invitations

Caroline Reutter—Foreword

Reynolds Tavern—Photography on page 29

© Jodi Roberts—Graphic design/line art and invitation for page 90

Stephanie Rose—Props

© Rose Street Design—Invitations for page 44

Meg Samek-Smith—Introduction

© Tinka. Image from BigStockPhoto.com—Photography on page 15

Lu Waters—Props

Hallie Wyrick—Props

Williams-Sonoma—Plates/props

RECIPE CONTRIBUTORS

We would like to recognize the following members, friends, and family of The Junior League of Annapolis, Inc. for graciously sharing their favorite recipes with us. Without their fabulous recipes, this book would not have been possible! We apologize if a name has been inadvertently omitted.

Gary Amoth	April Gremillion	Elaine Nagey
Jean Andrews	Ann Griffith	Pat Nagey
Liz Barclay	Mary Griffith	Melissa Niccoli
Kim Blitzer	Stephanie Griffith	Beth Niccolini
Wendy Bogarde	Mary "Maggi" Gunnels	Sandy Nuwar
Jane Bowen	Carrie Hilliard	Julie O'Donnell
Tina Bradley	Kimberly Hilliard	Dawn Orso
Dot Brugnoli	Anne Hopkins	Elaina O'Toole
Leigh Ellen Brummerhoff	Ena Laurie Kearns	Karen Paulin
Lee Perry Casey	Carolyn Keenen	Lila Perilloux
Pam Chaconas	Sherrie Kelley	Stephanie Pisarski
Gwen Clifford	Mary Kelly	Janet Porter
Beth Coleman	Luanne Kerrigan	Kate Riggs
Celia Coughlin	Amy Killila	Victoria Roberts
Susan Dahl	Laura Lane	Joyce Ronan
Barbara Davis	Laura LaRosa	Joan Ruch
Heather DeBuse	Melissa Marsden	Meg Samek-Smith
Kristin DeMarco	Holly McDermott	Nikki Schieke
Jill Derlink	Gretchen McKay	Pamela Shapiro
Louise Bell Devanny	Carole Mendez	Helen Sherman
Judy Diehl	Shannon Messick	Trisha Thomas
Nancy DiNunzio	Donna Metzger	Linda Underdown
Kelly Dovi	Marcia Meyers	Wendy Urban
Nellie Duke	Tammi Molavi	Morgan Van Arsdall
Kendel Erhlich	Dory Mondor	Victoria Vasenden
Debbie Fales	Stephanie Monrad	Gary Waters
Jennifer Filligin	Laura Moore	Lu Waters
Cindy Fischer	Anne Murphy	Hallie Wyrick
Erin Greco	Michele Murphy	Jennifer Zwartendijk

TEST KITCHEN HOSTESSES

We would like to thank the following Junior League of Annapolis members
for coordinating test kitchen parties and spending countless hours and dollars cooking,
testing, and evaluating the recipes for *A Thyme to Entertain*.

Jean Andrews

Jennifer Barrett

Dot Brugnoli

Leigh Ellen Brummerhoff

Angela Carbon-Clanton

Lee Perry Casey

Tammy Counts

Mary Diligent

Kelly Dovi

Melissa Fennelly

Amanda Finnis

Stephanie Griffith

Carrie Hilliard

Kimberly Hilliard

The Junior League of
    Annapolis Board of
    Directors 2006–2007

Mary Kelly

Luanne Kerrigan

Laura Lane

Kristi McCue

Holly McDermott

Gretchen McKay

Tammi Molavi

Anne Murphy

Dawn Orso

Mandy Owens

Bonnie Palsa

Janet Porter

Joan Ruch

Ianthe Saylor

Nikki Schieke

Pamela Shapiro

Helen Sherman

Suzanne Sudo

Tricia Ternovan

Karen Williams

Hallie Wyrick

SPONSORS & DONATIONS

The Junior League of Annapolis, Inc. would like to extend a personal thank you
to the following businesses and people in the community for their generous donations to
help support the production of *A Thyme to Entertain*.

SPONSORS

PICNIC BOAT LEVEL

Oreck Clean Home Center

SKIPJACK LEVEL

Jean Andrews, Champion Reality, Inc.
The Junior League of Annapolis Sustainers
Reynolds Tavern

LOG CANOE LEVEL

Annapolis Marriott Waterfront Hotel
National Carpet
The Westin Hotel Annapolis

DRAKETAIL LEVEL

The Junior League of Annapolis Board of Directors 2006–2007
Holly McDermott and Family

OTHER NOTABLE DONATIONS

Jean Andrews	Helen B. Gilbert	Greg and Mandy Owens
Mary Gale Buchanan	Russ and Stephanie Griffith	Joel and Carolyn Pugh
Wes and Marilyn Burge	Carolyn Kennen	Queenstown Bank of Maryland
Lee Perry Casey	Elizabeth H. Lasley	Schultz Family/Fisherman's Inn
Stephanie Clark	Kelly Mann	Meg Samek-Smith
Lysbeth Courtney	Matthew and Gretchen McKay	Wes and Helen Sherman
Joel and Kelly Dovi	Elizabeth Reeves Murphy	Laura Sullivan
Sven and Amanda Finnis	Brent and Diane Owens	Hallie Wyrick
	Donald and Louise Owens	

RESOURCE GUIDE

FOR THE HOME

THE CAIRN ANTIQUE SHOP
23 East Dover Street
Easton, MD 21601
410-822-2857

NATIONAL CARPET
Routes 2 and 214
Edgewater, MD 21037
410-956-9200
Route 3 South
Crofton, MD 21114
410-721-4747

ORECK CLEAN HOME CENTER
2138 Generals Highway #A
Annapolis, MD 21401
410-224-7500

PARKEMOOR HOME
175 Mitchell's Chance Road
Edgewater, MD 21037
410-956-1701
www.parkemoorhome.com

WILLIAMS-SONOMA
1705 Annapolis Mall
Annapolis, MD 21401
410-571-0589
www.williams-sonoma.com

GROUPS AND ORGANIZATIONS

ANNAPOLIS AND ANNE ARUNDEL COUNTY CONFERENCE AND VISITORS BUREAU
26 West Street
Annapolis, MD 21401
410-280-0445
www.visitannapolis.org

THE JUNIOR LEAGUE OF ANNAPOLIS, INC
134 Holiday Court
Suite 306
Annapolis, MD 21401
410-224-8984
www.jlannapolis.org

HOTELS AND RESORTS

ANNAPOLIS MARRIOTT WATERFRONT HOTEL
80 Compromise Street
Annapolis, MD 21401
410-268-7555
www.annapolismarriott.com

FISHERMAN'S INN
3116 Main Street
Grasonville, MD 21638
410-827-8807
www.fishermansinn.com

THE WESTIN ANNAPOLIS
100 Westgate Circle
Annapolis, MD 21401
410-972-4300
www.westin.com/annapolis

RESOURCE GUIDE

INVITATIONS

CHRISTIE PIRRUNG STATIONERY
WEDDING COORDINATOR
Stationery, Invitations and Gifts
12 Romar Drive
Annapolis, MD 21403
410-268-5158
cpirrungstationery@comcast.net

FOUR SEASONS PUBLISHING, INC.
www.fourseasonspub.com

GLAD TIDINGS, INC.
www.gladtidingspapers.com

LOVIE AND DODGE
www.lovieanddodge.com

ODD BALLS
www.oddballsinvitations.net

ROSE STREET DESIGN CO.
www.rosestreet.com

PHOTOGRAPHY AND VISUAL ART

BIG STOCK PHOTO
www.bigstockphoto.com

CHEF STEPHANIE ROSE
Food & Prop Styling
646-246-6072
www.foodstylings.com

DEAN ALEXANDER PHOTOGRAPHY
39 East Ostend Street
Baltimore, MD 21230
410-385-3120
www.deanalexander.com

OFF THE WALL
Artist: Jodi Roberts
443-867-8197
jmroberts27@hotmail.com

RESOURCE GUIDE

RESTAURANTS AND MARKETS

CAROLINE'S
1580 Whitehall Road
Annapolis, MD 21401
888-801-CAKE
www.carolinescakes.com

KOOL ICE & SEAFOOD CO.
110 Washington Street
Cambridge, MD 21613
410-228-2300
www.freshmarylandseafood.com

M. SLAVIN & SONS FISH
2710 South Glebe Road
Arlington, VA 22206
703-486-0400
www.mslavin.com

RESTAURANT EVE
110 South Pitt Street
Alexandria, VA 22314
703-706-0450
www.restauranteve.com

REYNOLDS TAVERN
7 Church Circle
Annapolis, MD 21401
410-295-9555
www.reynoldstavern.org

OTHER RESOURCES

JEAN ANDREWS, CHAMPION REALTY, INC.
Independent Contractor
541-A Baltimore Annapolis Boulevard
Severna Park, MD 21146
410-975-3286
www.jeanandrews.com

THE BALTIMORE SUN COMPANY
501 North Calvert Street
P.O. Box 1377
Baltimore, MD 21278
410-332-6000
www.baltimoresun.com

QUEENSTOWN BANK OF MARYLAND
7101 Main Street
P.O. Box 120
Queenstown, MD 21658
410-827-8881
www.queenstown-bank.com

INDEX

INDEX

INDEX

INDEX

INDEX